TOP GUN
PERFORMANCE

TOP GUN PERFORMANCE

From the Cockpit to the Boardroom

Ted Carter and Jack Stark

Potomac Books

An imprint of the University of Nebraska Press

Library of Congress Control Number: 2024048526

Set in Garamond Premier Pro by A. Shahan.

Contents

Illustrations

Figures

Acknowledgments

Special thank you to Jane Ferreyra and Taylor Gilreath at the University of Nebraska Press. Appreciation to psychiatrist Dr. Chris Kratochvil and psychologist Dr. Steph Koraleski for their extraordinary editorial contributions and recommendations.

Appreciation to all the men and women who served on flight decks—the most dangerous four and a half acres of steel—in all the navy.

—Vice Admiral Carter

To all my patients, clients, and mentees who have enriched my life. A special recognition to my wife, Shirley Stark, for all her hundreds of hours of work on this book.

—Dr. Stark

TOP GUN
PERFORMANCE

PART 1

TOP GUN

The Need for Top Gun Performance

Ah, but a man's reach should exceed his grasp, or what's a heaven for?
—ROBERT BROWNING

Top Gun, or exceptional, performance may seem an elusive goal or something that is achievable by only a gifted few, but it is completely within your grasp. You may want to get a promotion at work, or take some time off your 5K run, or be more emotionally available to your partner or children; Top Gun performance in your life may look totally different from exceptional performance in someone else's life. What will be the same for everyone is learning how to use their mental and physical resources to reach for those higher heights. Let's try an experiment—please follow these instructions:

1. Raise your hand as high as you can.
2. Now pause for a few seconds.
3. Now raise it higher!

Were you able to raise your hand a couple inches higher? We have made this request of thousands of individuals who we have presented to and, without fail, the audience members are able to raise their hands a little higher, without much effort, all in response to our simple request. When you raise your hand those extra few inches, that is the 5 percent difference in action. Imagine what would happen if you were able to make that kind of improvement in your daily life—school, sports, work.

Now also imagine that we were able to maximize our BODY and our MIND to promote a really noticeable elite performance.

Building a National Championship Dynasty—
the 5 Percent Difference

The above exercise demonstrates the power of the 5 percent difference on performance. What if you, your team, or your company could achieve a 5 percent improvement to the bottom line? That's the difference between winning and losing, between contributing to a profitable year for your company or losing your job.

Think of the 2016–17 year in sports. A 5 percent difference allowed

1. the Cubs to win the World Series,
2. the Cavs to come back from three games down and win the NBA championship, and
3. the Patriots to come back from twenty-five points down to win the Super Bowl.

Flying an F-18 at Mach speed, conducting combat sorties, or landing on a moving aircraft carrier at night leaves little room for error.

JACK STARK'S 5 PERCENT STORY

In 1989, after giving a presentation to the University of Nebraska's football coaching staff to see if they wanted to hire me, I (Jack Stark) had a one-on-one meeting with the head coach, Tom Osborne. I was excited but nervous. Here was my childhood hero who had grown up in the same small Nebraska town of Hastings as I did, had been the state and college athlete of the year, attended a seminary for religious training, and acquired his PhD in psychology in the same department as I did at the University of Nebraska. We had a lot in common, and I was eager to make a good impression and, I hoped, be hired as team psychologist. I clearly remember telling him, "Coach, I don't want to overpromise what I can do for the team—I think I can make only a 5 percent difference." Dr. Osborne looked at me and said, "Jack, do you know what you are talking about? A 5 percent difference at this level of college football is huge—it's the difference of a national championship."

In the decade before I arrived, the Nebraska football team had won 82.5 percent of its games. In the decade I was there in the 1990s we won 88.5 percent of our games with three national championships and nine conference championships, and we had a record of 60-3 over the course of five years. In the two decades after I left, the Huskers won only 50 percent of their games.

As the team psychologist for the Nebraska Husker football team from 1989 to 2003, I was blessed to experience the 5 percent difference phenomenon. This accomplishment was the result of recruiting faster players, making defense changes, and the head coach's embracing a focus on team unity and the importance of the mental game!

Our 1995 team was voted by *Sports Illustrated* as the fourth-best sports team of all time. First was the 1927 Yankees; second, the 1977 Montreal Canadiens; third, the 1985 Chicago Bears; and fourth, the 1995 Nebraska Husker football team. The 1995 football team beat its opponents by thirty-six points a game and defeated four top-ten teams. It is still considered the best college football team in the modern era.

What we, as part of the entire Nebraska football staff, did for our Nebraska football players is the same thing that we applied to other teams in winning a total of twenty-two national championships and establishing dynasties that lasted for many years in NASCAR, collegiate football, and collegiate wrestling, and among Olympic gold and silver medalists.

Similarly we used the same team-focus approach and body-mind skill techniques when we coached individuals, corporations, Fortune 500 companies, and small businesses. In addition the thousands of patients who came to see us made tremendous gains with successful outcomes.

We found similar results with our other elite athletes who won national championships in their sports, earned medals in the Olympics, or became exceptional leaders in the military and in corporate settings.

How Can I Get Better? Inspiration Performance Films

Knute Rockne—All-American (1940). Coach Knute Rockne gave his "Win one for the Gipper" speech to the Notre Dame players at halftime of the 1928 Army game. Rockne was trying to salvage something from his worst season as a coach at Notre Dame. To inspire his players, he told them the story of the tragic death of the greatest player ever at Notre Dame, George Gipp.

In the movie, the scene between Rockne and Gipp was the first of three classic locker-room scenes. Rockne was played by the venerable actor Pat O'Brien, and Gipp was played by Ronald Reagan.

Rockne: "Well, boys . . . I haven't a thing to say. Played a great game thus far—all of you. Great game.

"I guess we can't expect to win 'em all. I'm going to tell you something I've kept to myself for years—none of you ever knew Gipp. It was long before your time. But you know what a tradition he is at Notre Dame. And the last thing he said to me, 'Rock, sometime when the team is up against it—and the breaks are beating the boys—tell them to go out there with all they got and win just one for the Gipper.'"

Notre Dame went on to beat Army.

Hoosiers (1986). Actor Gene Hackman plays the coach of a small Indiana town's high school basketball team. Hickory High, with an enrollment of only 161 students, won the 1954 Indiana state championship against bigger schools. *Hoosiers* has been voted the greatest basketball movie of all time.

Coach: "If you put your effort and concentration into playing to your potential, to be the best that you can be, I don't care what the scoreboard says at the end of the game; in my book, we're gonna be winners."

Player: "Let's win this game for all the small schools that never had a chance to get here."

Any Given Sunday (1999). This movie's half-time locker-room speech by Al Pacino as the head coach to the mythical Miami Sharks, an NFL team, is considered by many critics to be one of the top-ten inspirational speeches of all time.

"I don't know what to say really.

"Three minutes to the biggest battle of our professional lives—all comes down to today.

"Now either we heal as a team or we're gonna crumble.

"Inch by inch.

"Play by play.

"'Til we're finished.

"You find out life's this game of inches. So is football. Because in either game—life or football—the margin for error is so small.

"I mean, one half-step too late or too early and you don't quite make it; one half-second too slow, too fast, you don't quite catch it.

"The inches we need are everywhere around us.

"They're in every break of the game, every minute, every second.

"On this team, we fight for that inch.

"On this team, we tear ourselves and everyone else around us to pieces for that inch.

"We claw with our fingernails for the inch!

"Because we know when we add up all the inches, that's gonna make all the difference between winning and losing!

"Between living and dying.

"I'll tell you this: in any fight, it's the guy who's willing to die who's gonna win that inch.

"And I know, if I'm gonna have any life anymore, it's because I'm still willing to fight and die for that inch.

"Because that's what living is!"

These three bits of movie dialog capture the essence of this book. Exceptional students, athletes, military personnel, and business leaders and individuals seeking to maximize their daily performance ask:

"How can I get better?"

How can I maximize my talent? How can I achieve exceptional performance in my daily life? In my work? And in my physical performance? We often use the mantra "One player, one play, one game." The authors of this book have been part of teams that have won or lost national championships on one play by one player in one game. Remember, up to fifty different football players are involved in over 150 plays in twelve to twenty games from college to the NFL.

One rogue leader can engage in unethical behavior on any given day, and it can bring down an entire country, army, or Fortune 100 company as happened at Enron. Or an individual can save an entire country (Winston Churchill).

One person can find a cure for polio (Jonas Salk).

One person can inspire the entire world (Martin Luther King Jr., Mother Teresa).

An individual who can harness the power of their body and their mind can have a huge impact on their own lives and, potentially, the lives of others.

Why the Usual Approach to Performance Training Fails

We live in a competitive world where every little advantage is magnified. We see such competition in corporations who are constantly looking for an edge over the competition—that 5 percent difference that will make them successful in their field. Corporations strive for that difference via inventive branding of their products and services, cutting-edge marketing, and innovation that will give consumers "gotta have" hot products.

In their personal lives, individuals strive for being better whether it is by following the latest diet fad, slaving away at the gym, using liposuction or plastic surgery to improve appearance, or adhering to a supplement-and-vitamin regimen to look and feel better. People read books, listen to podcasts, and attend seminars on how to improve their work ethic, their parenting, or their relationships. Unfortunately, if they never get to their personal or professional goals, many tend to blame themselves, but what is really happening is that those dispensing the advice are deficient in their training, experience, and, most of all, leadership skills.

BARRIERS TO SUCCESS

We in leadership and training positions fail to develop Top Gun performers because we often fail to "give our skills away" due to *barriers*.

We will never have enough *time, money, staff*, or *equipment*. We have too many people to train with short-term results and often politics. These barriers are everywhere and are the essence of failure.

We must give our skills away so that others have self-control across all settings.

We offer six audio files for Top Gun performers to download onto their phones to help readers maximize their performance—from stress reduction to optimizing sleep. Each audio file is accompanied by a chapter to augment our readers' learning.

Case Studies

Following are three case studies of individuals we have consulted with in the past regarding performance issues. These three are representative of the thousands of individuals who have benefited from our combined interventions.

DEPRESSED

A forty-eight-year-old prominent attorney was referred for treatment of depression. Her OB/GYN was concerned about her fatigue, sleep issues, lack of interest in previous hobbies, poor concentration, and other symptoms typical of depression.

Like a good clinician, I documented the patient's history. Her law practice was thriving, her marriage was good, her kids were happy, and she had no genetic history of depression.

The typical approach, some thirty years ago, was to prescribe for her the promising new medication Prozac. But nothing seemed to point to depression as a cause of her symptoms. A quick and simple approach would have been to try the medication and come back in three to four weeks to see how much progress had been made.

Instead, I suggested she go back to her OB/GYN and ask him to repeat the lab test that he ordered six months earlier. A real long shot!

Sure enough, he called me and said, "Wow! I am amazed that the new scores are abnormal. How did you know?" Lab scores do not usually change that fast in six months. Guilt quickly followed as I wondered how many individuals we had treated with antidepressants over the years when symptoms were actually changes in lab results. Perhaps this problem with diagnosis explains why today one in four women aged eighteen to forty in this country has been or will be prescribed an antidepressant.

HITTING THE WALL

At an upscale fitness studio, we conducted a small informal study. The savvy owner came to us saying he was running into a frequent problem with his members. The physicians, attorneys, and former elite athletes were "hitting the wall" despite consistent intensive training. They exhibited the typical symptoms of "metabolic syndrome," a cluster of conditions including weight gain, abdominal fat, high cholesterol and triglyceride levels, blood pressure elevation, and symptoms of what seemed to be low levels of depression due to stress.

Before prescribing extensive testing for depression or other issues, a team member suggested a preliminary lab blood testing protocol. The findings revealed that twenty-eight of the forty individuals evaluated had low or very low hormone levels. The results were consistent even for a few individuals in their late twenties.

Medical treatment significantly improved scores.

The fitness center changed its strategies and approaches to improving health among its members and now provides medical care for body-mind enhancement.

Once again, we avoided the wrong treatment path.

A DIFFERENT APPROACH TO SUCCESS

NASCAR, or stock car auto racing, is a sport we have been very active in consulting via long-term, multiyear support of many top teams.

We won and we lost championships by inches, by tenths of seconds. A physician and I together watched a race where a championship driver and his team suffered an exceedingly bad day. The pit crew, driver, and support staff all struggled in a key midseason race. In a postrace phone consultation with the team, we offered recommendations. Our protocol included specific hydration recommendations, as drivers and pit crew team members can lose up to eight pounds of fluid on a hot race day lasting four or more hours. Success! The team performed admirably and won a key race the next weekend.

What would *not* have been successful is one of the typical responses such as calling a team meeting or getting after the crew.

The critical performance of an individual or team is dependent on selecting the exact approach for producing an exceptional performance while avoiding traditional quick fixes.

How Do We Reach Exceptional Top Gun Performance?

Improving the body while improving the mind is an example of the math formula 2 + 2 = 5 or the Gestalt philosophy "the whole is greater than the sum of its parts."

Simultaneously improving the mind and the body has a maximizing effect.

An example of this maximizing effect took place in 1990 when the University of Nebraska football team, which we were a part of, lost badly in the Citrus Bowl to Georgia Tech, who went on to become national champions. An appeal was made to Nebraska's coaching staff to make major changes.

Physically they recruited speed over size. All the positions became smaller but faster. Strength, better training, and style of play were updated and drastically changed. Most important, we implemented a team unity program called the Unity Council: a weekly meeting with players to promote unity among everyone—players, coaches, and staff. The result was that after a couple of years building the program, we went 60-3 over a five-year period with three national championships and nine conference championships—more than the previous eighty years combined.

With the same body, we can significantly improve and enhance our physical and mental performances. Through technology, nutrition, training programs, and body-mind research, we can advance body-mind performance.

The mind (our thinking and reaction to our daily experiences) is processed in the brain, which within a tenth of a second sends signals to our endocrine system—hormones—to prepare us for "fight or flight," resulting in more than 1,200 chemical changes.

This process stresses our bodies (cortisol, fatigue), prematurely ages us, and causes health problems that we can now better measure via brain scans and lab work.

A Body-Mind Message from Warren Buffett

Warren Buffett gave the best presentation on the important role of the body-mind connection on performance.

In 2003 a colleague, David Sokol, was kind enough to arrange for two local Omaha billionaires, Warren Buffett and Walter Scott Jr., to talk to the entire Nebraska Husker football team and staff just before a big game.

The players and staff were eager to hear from the local billionaire Buffett, whose net worth was ranked in the top three worldwide.

Buffett told the football players he wanted to do something special for them, as he had graduated from Nebraska U.

He told the team that he was going to buy each player a new car, any car they wanted: Rolls-Royce, Lamborghini, Maserati—anything. He paused, and the players were going wild, high-fiving each other and laughing as they really started to believe he was going to do that; after all, he could easily afford it out of his $60 billion net worth. As I sat in the back of the room with the players, I began to panic—thinking that would be illegal in the NCAA and we would all get in trouble.

Then Warren dropped the bomb. He said that there was only one catch to buying them whatever car they wanted.

He said that the condition is that this would be the *only* car they could ever have for the rest of their lives.

A puzzled look and furrowed foreheads replaced their giddy laughter.

He said, "That's right. The condition is that this car, again whatever you want, would be the only car you would drive for the rest of your life."

The team's disappointment, however, turned into their acknowledgment of a life lesson, their heads nodding when he said, "You see, guys, that new car is like your body. You get only one car, or one body, and you have to take really good care of your body for the rest of your life." That story stayed with the team, and many changed the way they treated their bodies from that day forward.

We also went on to win that game.

Our mantra is "One player, one play, one game can win or lose an entire season or championship" (World Series champions Chicago Cubs, 2016). One person, one transaction, one day can bankrupt a large multibillion-dollar company as well (Enron, Lehman Brothers, and Bear Stearns had some of the biggest bankruptcies in U.S. history).

NASCAR teams we consulted with won and lost national championships by one-tenth of a second in a race or by one-tenth of a percent over a thirty-six-race season.

And so, this small difference of 2–5 percent is the same for all of us. EVERYONE wants to WIN! But winning is difficult. This level of difficulty seems to be growing as the speed and complexity of competition continue to grow each year. We all want to be appreciated, respected, and happy. Or as the psychologist Abraham Maslow found, we want to reach our highest level of satisfaction—self-fulfillment!

In practical terms, it means we want to win in all areas of our lives: SCHOOL, SPORTS, and WORK.

People and particularly leaders want to know the how, when, where, what, and, most important, why of winning. The levels of dissatisfaction, discontent, and depression are at an all-time high. From 9/11 in 2001 to the financial melt-down in 2008–10, we witnessed a decade with many more failures than win-ners. We witnessed the biggest bankruptcies in U.S. history among companies that everyone once touted as the best in the world in their respective fields.

People want answers, specific ones—not some theory or personal view from someone who has never competed at the highest level or won a championship.

We were told "good" is the enemy of "great"! But it turned out that "great" wasn't so great after all. Of the 1,400 companies Jim Collins studied in his book *Good to Great*, only eleven met the criterion of a stock return three times that of the market over a fifteen-year period during the 1980s and 1990s.

It turns out that none survived the past two decades to meet this criterion, even barely. Many went bankrupt, and two of them (Fannie and Freddie) needed a $200 billion TARP bailout.

This is why we decided to tell our story—a story of witnessing exceptional performance. Our approach is based on our combined seventy years of expe-riences, research, analyses, and successes and failures.

We have consulted with world leaders, corporate teams, and elite athletes. Our perspective is that of a performance psychologist and a distinguished Top Gun pilot.

Our behind-the-scenes stories, techniques, and analyses provide a blueprint for building your own exceptional performance. Reviewing our lifework with some successful outcomes offers our readers a design they can replicate in their lifework.

By participating in this journey with us, you will learn a lot about yourself, those around you, and the teams that you are part of to help you reach your highest level of performance.

We live in a world now obsessed with performance. We hear phrases like, "It is all about your performance," "It is the bottom line that counts," "It is, what have you done for me lately?" "It is the wins and losses that count."

Pay, *power*, and *prestige* too often, unfortunately, appear to be the three main motivators in our lives that drive us to be better. They are used as a basis of our evaluation system—grades, work evaluations, annual performance reviews, wins, and losses.

The word "performance" is one of the most googled words in the English language, with "stress" being the most popular searched title. Stress is code for

"How can I perform better?" each day. Regardless of our age, gender, talent, attractiveness, IQ, or EQ we all have the capacity to perform better.

The authors of this book, due to great mentors, are blessed to be able to spend our professional lives focused on how we can help others perform better both physically and mentally.

Early Career Challenges: Stark

After college and midway through graduate school in the early 1970s, I was eager to change the world by teaching inner-city students, supporting families, and treating students with severe behavioral issues.

My idealism was severely challenged when I was hired to work with more than one hundred severely challenged students in a large public school system—all by myself.

Eager to please, I served those students and their families in the first three months of the school year and found one hundred more referrals in my inbox that needed immediate attention.

I made a visit to a teacher who demanded that I remove a student who exhibited a typical behavior problem. When I informed the teacher that I had nowhere to place the student, particularly outside the home or the school district, she blamed me and suggested I was no help and refused to develop a treatment program that we had success with.

That's when it hit me. I shouted to myself, I am better than this, I have overachieved, yet the need is overwhelming, I must devise a better way.

I learned, as many of you have perhaps also learned, you have

1. not enough time,
2. not enough money,
3. not enough staff,
4. not enough equipment,
5. so many people to help in need of service,
6. only short-term results in changing behavior, and
7. political issues that present challenges.

As a result of this experience, I developed a philosophy of "giving away our skills" to as many people as we can. The old adage still applies: "if I give you a fish you can eat today—if I teach you how to fish you can eat for life."

This desire to teach others to have "self-control" was reinforced by research among adolescents with behavioral problems, a private practice of ten thousand patients, and consulting to more than one hundred companies and approximately eight thousand athletes at some fifty colleges and universities and on professional and Olympic teams.

These experiences taught us that we needed to develop a system of helping others to change without being dependent on us or others all the time.

We wanted to teach leaders how they can best lead, athletes how to work on skills that they can practice on their own, and patients, clients, coaches, pilots, and mentors how to use material we developed because there will never be enough staff, money, or facilities and will always be way too many people who need help. We even specifically developed material for high school coaches on how to be a "Top Gun performer for under $50." That's because it's coming out of their pockets, and that's all they could afford.

All social systems are overwhelmed today. Schools, churches, social agencies, military leaders, physicians, psychologists, and families are stressed to the max, and until we can find a better way to help others to better help themselves the performance issues will only get worse.

Challenges to Performance

It is often difficult to know how to perform better in today's complex world. If you ask yourself "What is a hard choice?" and "What is an easy choice?" you will find your answer.

The problem today is too many people want easy choices.

Many years ago, I had an opportunity to ask the most influential psychologist to ever live, B. F. Skinner, what the biggest problem is that we have as a society, and his answer was profound.

He stated, "Jack, the main problem with people all over the world is that they have an inability to delay gratification. It's built into our DNA. The 'I want it now' syndrome."

We eat too much, drink too much, spend and consume too much. The result is a world with growing anger, loneliness, and unhappiness, all of which have a significant impact on our performance behaviors.

ANGER

It's an ironic phenomenon that our standard of living keeps improving each decade, yet our stress levels, anger, unhappiness, and loneliness are growing even faster. Many people provide the following answers:

It's the bad economy—the growing gap between the haves
    and the have-nots.
The lack of stability in the home.
The inability of teachers and parents to instill manners in
    young children.
The intrusiveness of the government.
The chemicals in our food.
The anonymity of the internet.
Reality TV and violence in the media.
The 24-hour news cycle with scary news.
The increasing polarization of political parties.
The shrinking global economy.
Conflict everywhere—pandemics.
Social media—the expression of anger that gets reinforced
    and grows over small things from work to sports and to
    daily living activities.

Anger and aggression have always been around, and there is never going to be a complete end to violence. But we can and need to control it (Whitbourne 2010).

One neuroscientist who has studied why anger causes people to become violent states, "It's anger, not religion or politics that is the root cause of terrorism across the globe, it's huge and it's growing" (Fields 2016).

In a survey conducted by *Esquire* and NBC News in 2016 roughly half of Americans said they're angrier than they used to be and nearly seven out of ten said they're angered by something in the news at least once a day. The National Institutes of Health says more than 16 million Americans have a condition called "intermittent explosive disorder," also known as "road rage," in which people get angry out of proportion with the circumstances.

The neuroscientist mentioned above indicates that the world is creating more anger, sudden aggression, and more violence because our brains are operating in an environment they were never designed to operate in, and we have developed crowded living environments where we constantly push on these triggers (Graham 2017).

The American Psychological Association indicates that 90 percent of aggressive incidents are preceded by anger. Only 10 percent of anger experiences, however, are actually followed by aggression.

Anger has many negative consequences for our work, relationships, family interactions, and areas of performance. It takes an enormous toll on our bodies (e.g., heart disease) and our minds, as we point out in the following chapters.

LONELINESS

To say that loneliness is an epidemic in the United States is an understatement. Social scientists have discovered that the prevalence of loneliness has more than doubled in the United States in the past fifty years. It now affects 42 million Americans over age forty-five.

Loneliness is a gap between the kind of social relations you want and what you actually have. It's a perception one has versus the number of people around you.

A meta-analysis (summary findings) of seventy studies showed that loneliness increases the risk of death by 26 percent. This makes loneliness as great a public health risk as obesity. Isolation increases our risk of chronic body inflammation, which can lead to high blood pressure, diabetes, cancer, and cognitive decline (*Social Isolation and Loneliness* 2020).

Good relationships improve our satisfaction with life and give us a sense of meaning and purpose—what, the Dalai Lama says, makes us truly happy in life.

A study of 1,981 heterosexual couples led by researchers at Michigan State (Health Psychology) found that happy spouses have better health, live longer, and exercise and eat right.

Jobs with the highest suicide rates were construction and farming—both involve stressful work environments, isolation, and less access to mental health services (Centers for Disease Control and Prevention, *Morbidity and Mortality Weekly Report*, 2018).

Economists and public health experts consider life expectancy to be an important measure of a nation's prosperity.

Data from a recent Centers for Disease Control and Prevention report show a disturbing finding. Life expectancy has fallen in the past few years after centuries of rising to the high seventies. This change reflects the effects of addictions (opioids) and despair on higher suicide rates, particularly among middle-aged adults. COVID and its impact also played a dramatic role in this finding.

While we have made some amazing progress against heart disease and cancer—the number one and number two causes of death—anger, loneliness, and the lack of happiness are really our biggest challenge for the future.

What eats away at our happiness?

A recent Harris Poll on happiness indicated that only one in three Americans report being very happy. There are declines in one's sense of purpose, strength of our relationships, and physical and financial health.

This unhappiness has been on the rise for the last decade. One senior pastor (Floyd 2018) believes there are five emotional diseases that eat away at our happiness and health:

1. ingratitude,
2. entitlement,
3. discontentedness,
4. criticism, and
5. cynicism.

What Motivates Us

Many years ago, I worked as a consultant for over a decade with a large manufacturing company that employed five thousand workers making electronic equipment. As part of an international corporation, we were often asked to do sophisticated surveys put together by a panel of PhD experts. The results were often confusing and pointless but made a certain group feel like they were contributing.

The plant manager of the organization did something that surprised and humbled me.

A quiet, respected man, he asked me to randomly video record a hundred employees and ask them one simple question: "What motivates you?"

Skeptical at first, I was amazed at the response and success of this simple question. People wanted to be heard, and they appreciated that, but more important, they talked about being appreciated and the support and friendship of their colleagues.

It was not about money, perks, complaints, working conditions—it was about what makes you happy and motivated.

Psychologists often cite the famous psychologist Abraham Maslow, who over eighty years ago explained his theory of motivation. He described a pyramid-shaped hierarchy ranging from the bottom need—biological (air, food, drink)—to the highest level of self-actualization and self-fulfillment and the transference of that to others.

Maslow pointed out correctly that only one in one hundred actually reach this highest level, as we get "stuck" in the lower levels of motivational needs.

"Where there is patience and humility there is neither anger nor vexation" are the wise words of St. Francis of Assisi.

1. Official vice admiral portrait taken for new position as superintendent, U.S. Naval Academy, July 2014. Courtesy Ted Carter.

2. ABOVE: Flight instructor duty with student Tomcat pilot at Otis Air National Guard Base in Cape Cod, June 1988. This particular Tomcat from the VF-124 Gunfighters was an air show bird. Courtesy Ted Carter.

3. Carter's Top Gun (Navy Fighter Weapons School) graduation plaque from March 1985. There is no such thing as a Top Gun trophy; this is what actual Top Gun graduates receive upon successful completion of the Top Gun program. Courtesy Ted Carter.

4. Official portrait upon departing duties as president, U.S. Naval War College, in Newport, Rhode Island, July 2014. Carter was the fifty-fourth president in War College history dating back to 1888 with the first two presidents, Rear Admiral Stephen Luce and Rear Admiral Alfred Thayer Mahan. Created by Gerald Slater. Courtesy Ted Carter.

5. Strapped into an F-14A Tomcat during flight instructor duty with the VF-124 Gunfighters. Carter would become the flight instructor of the year in 1987. He always considered the backseat of the F-14 Tomcat to be his office. Carter would eventually end his career with over 6,100 flying hours in tactical jet aircraft, including over 4,400 hours in the Tomcat (second-most all-time for Tomcat aviators). Courtesy Ted Carter.

6. Official portrait from service as sixty-second superintendent, U.S. Naval Academy, 2014–19. Carter was the longest continuously serving superintendent at Annapolis since the Civil War. The portrait is hung in Dahlgren Hall, where he had played ice hockey from 1977 to 1981 as a midshipman. Created by Gerald Slater. Courtesy Ted Carter.

7. ABOVE: Captain of the Navy ice hockey team, January 1981. Selected as the team's most valuable player in 1981 after leading the team in scoring (goals and assists). Courtesy Ted Carter.

8. OPPOSITE TOP: F-4 Phantom II in full afterburner, 1985. The Phantom was Carter's first fleet aircraft. He flew in it with over one thousand flight hours and attended Top Gun in the last all-Phantom class in March 1985. Courtesy Ted Carter.

9. Actual tailhook point from the F/A-18F Super Hornet for Carter's record-breaking two thousandth carrier-arrested landing on board USS *Enterprise* (CVN-65), October 3, 2012. Carter's pilot was Lieutenant Commander Jacob Rosales from Fighter Squadron VFA-11, the world-famous Red Rippers. VFA-11 removed the tailhook and did this wonderful artistic paint job for the historic keepsake. In the history of U.S. naval aviation, Carter remains the only aviator (of any designator) with two thousand carrier-arrested landings. His first landing was with Commander Bud Taylor onboard USS *Kitty Hawk* (CV-63) on August 20, 1983. Courtesy Ted Carter.

10. RIGHT: Carter's freshman or plebe portrait at Navy, August 1977. Courtesy Ted Carter.

11. The entire ready room of pilots and selected flight deck crew from Fighter Squadron 211, the Checkmates, onboard USS *Enterprise* (CVN-65), April 3, 2012. A trap is a carrier-arrested landing. The long-standing previous record had been 1,888 traps. Carter was a one-star admiral at the time and was serving as the *Enterprise* carrier strike group commander. Courtesy Ted Carter.

Congratulations, RDML Carter
On Your Record-Breaking Trap

1,889 TRAPS
APRIL 3, 2012

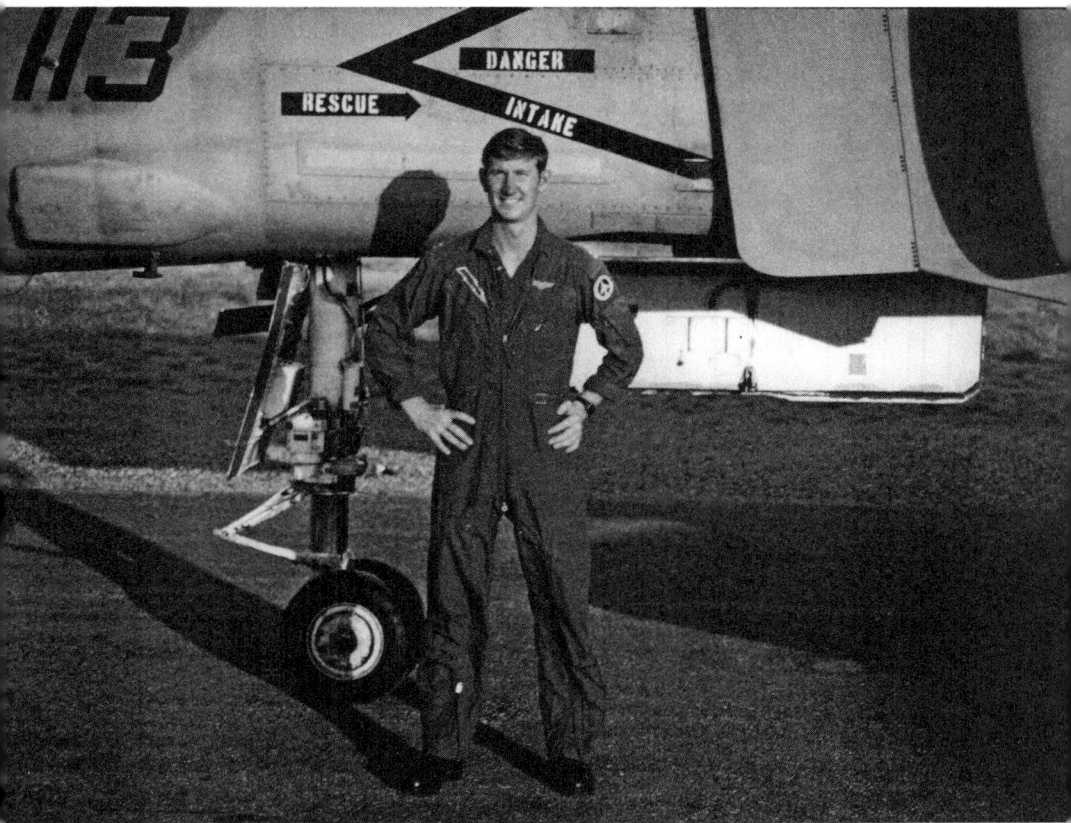

12. The last few days flying in the F-4S Phantom II. Carter flew twelve Phantoms from Fighter Squadrons VF-161 and VF-151 from Atsugi, Japan, to Davis-Monthan Air Force Base (affectionately known as the Boneyard). The transpacific flight had stops in Guam and Hawaii, and then into Arizona for the final stop. This image was taken at sunrise at Kaneohe Marine Corps Air Station, Hawaii, April 1986. Courtesy Ted Carter.

13. ABOVE: Selfie from the back seat of the F-4S Phantom II during operations over the South China Sea, February 1986. Courtesy Ted Carter.

14. Top Gun photo with Carter's Top Gun pilot, Lieutenant Rory Banks, March 1985. The entire class of eight fighter crews flew Phantoms, the final Top Gun class of all Phantoms. The *Top Gun* movie had just started filming. Courtesy Ted Carter.

15. Family photo with Carter and wife, Lynda, and their two children, Chris and Brittany. This was the day of taking command of VF-14, the Tophatters, flying the F-14A Tomcat in December 1998. Courtesy Ted Carter.

16. In command of vf-14, the Tophatters, circa 1999 after a unique combat deployment. vf-14 along with squadrons in Carrier Air Wing Eight deployed aboard uss *Theodore Roosevelt* (cvn 71) for over eight months to two combat theaters of operation: fifty-five days of combat in Operation Allied Force (Kosovo) and thirty-three days of combat in Iraq. Courtesy Ted Carter.

17. Hanging with Steven Tyler and Joe Perry and band members from Aerosmith, summer 2002. They made a welcome visit to USS *Harry S. Truman* (CVN 75) in Norfolk, Virginia, while Carter was second in command (executive officer). The first song at their concert in Virginia Beach was dedicated to Captain Ted "Slapshot" Carter and the crew: "Living on the Edge." Courtesy Ted Carter.

18. ABOVE: Attending a fundraiser with General Colin Powell while commanding USS *Carl Vinson* (CVN 70), Washington DC, November 4, 2008, the night President Obama was elected. Courtesy Ted Carter.

19. OPPOSITE TOP: Desert Storm photo taken after deployment in February 1991 by Commander Chuck "Heater" Heatly, who commanded the VF-21 Freelancers and is the pilot in the photo along with Carter. Heater did much of the filming and photography for the original *Top Gun* movie and was a Top Gun instructor himself. They flew together for their eight hundredth, nine hundredth, and one thousandth carrier-arrested landings, all aboard USS *Independence* (CV-62). Courtesy Ted Carter.

20. Lynda and Carter at USNA graduation and commissioning, Navy Marine Corps Memorial Stadium in Annapolis, May 27, 1981. They were engaged later that year on September 13 and married on July 31, 1982, while Carter was in flight school. Courtesy Ted Carter.

21. Representing a small cadre of retired military officers who were presidents or chancellors of a university or college by serving as the eighth president of the University of Nebraska system, October 2020. Courtesy Ted Carter.

22. In the Oval Office with President Trump briefing him on May 24, 2018, the day before he arrived and delivered the commencement address at USNA in Annapolis on May 25, 2018. The call to brief the president before the graduation and commissioning was unusual. The president wanted to know the history of the event and many of the details. It was Carter's first and only visit to the Oval Office. Courtesy Ted Carter.

2

The Top Gun Experience

If I have seen further, it is by standing on the shoulders of Giants.
—SIR ISAAC NEWTON, 1675

This quotation epitomizes how fortunate we have been to have exceptional leaders and experiences in our lives that have forever changed who we are and what we have accomplished.

In the highly successful movie series *Band of Brothers*, about a group of young men led by Lieutenant Winters during the invasion of Normandy in World War II, a comment by the lieutenant after the war captures the experience I, Ted Carter, had as a Top Gun graduate, F-14 Tomcat instructor, and career naval aviator: "In thinking back on the days of Easy Company, I'm treasuring my remark to a grandson who asked, 'Grandpa, were you a hero in the war?'

"'No,' I answered, 'but I served in a company of heroes.'"

I was honored to serve with an elite group of young men in Top Gun training and in each of the 125 combat missions I flew. I look forward to sharing these life experiences with my granddaughter.

Let me share with you the Top Gun program, how I got selected, what it was like to go through this elite experience, and how it changed and prepared me to be successful for the rest of my life.

Top Gun

In the 1950s, the U.S. Navy air-to-air combat training program called Fleet Air Gunnery Units provided air combat training to naval aviators.

In the 1960s the thinking of aerial combat shifted to long-range missile training. It was wrongly determined that air-to-air dogfights were obsolete, as missiles with radar and fire-control technology were all that was needed to engage with an adversary miles away. But there was a high rate of missile malfunction, and the need for tight maneuvering and agile fighting was critical during the Vietnam War.

In 1968 the chief of naval operations ordered the establishment of the Navy Fighter Weapons School due to the one thousand U.S. aircraft losses in one million sorties. The school, at Miramar, California, became known as Top Gun. The purpose was to train the best of the best fighter air crews at the graduate level in fighter weapons, tactics, techniques, and procedures.

Every instructor was an expert in training techniques. All lectures were given without notes. The training was intense.

An analysis of World War II pilots' records showed that only 4 percent of pilots accounted for 40 percent of the enemy aircraft destroyed. In the late 1960s, to duplicate this World War II achievement, Top Gun's approach resulted in a sixfold increase in combat success against enemy aircraft destroyed during Vietnam.

In 1995 the program was moved to Fallon, Nevada, and in 2016, it was rebranded as the Naval Aviation Warfighting Development Center, where Top Gun remains alongside graduate-level weapons schools today.

The school was made famous by the 1986 film *Top Gun* and its sequel, *Top Gun: Maverick*, in 2022.

Top Gun Training I: Flying the Phantom

I graduated from the U.S. Naval Academy in May 1981. I was selected for naval flight officer training and went to Pensacola, Florida, in the early fall of 1981. After about a year of flight training, I earned my naval aviation wings of gold in October 1982. It was at that point that I was selected for fighter jets. Now, in those days, naval aviators and naval flight officers really had two choices. You could be selected for training with either the F-14 Tomcat, which was a relatively new jet, or the aging Vietnam era of a jet aircraft, the F-4 Phantom. The F-4 Phantom was in its last years of operational use in the U.S. Navy. I was surprised, even though I finished number two in my flight class of over twenty-five fighter naval flight officers, that I was selected for F-4 Phantoms. It was my first lesson in accepting an outcome I had not requested. I learned not only to manage it but to turn it into an advantage.

I actually thought my career was over because I was assigned to this older-type model series aircraft. Before I transferred to my first fleet squadron, I went to a training squadron. In this case, I went to the F-4S fleet replacement squadron, VF-171, the Flying Aces, who were stationed at Naval Air Station Oceana, Master Jet Base, in Virginia. Oceana was packed with hundreds of airplanes on the flight line, about three-quarters of them Tomcats, the rest being A-6 Intruder bomber aircraft and the last remnant of the F-4 Phantom. This was during the Cold War, when tensions between Western countries and the Soviet Union were high. So, as I reflect on just that roughly nine months of training that I had in the F-4S Phantom II before I went to my fleet squadron, I realize how much of my aviation reputation was formed even at that early stage. In the "you can't make this up" category, the second flight I ever had in the F-4S Phantom II was noteworthy. I was crewed with a former helicopter pilot who had transitioned to be an F-4 pilot. I'll just use his call sign, which was Chopper. As we took the runway in April 1983, we were all set for what was supposed to be a normal familiarization flight. This flight was designed to go out and fly over the East Coast, fly over the ocean, and get used to the Phantom's basic flying parameters.

ARE YOU STILL WITH ME?

We always dropped our separate clamshell canopies in the F-4 Phantom together before takeoff just because it was always smart to look good. As we took the runway, ran the engines up, and came off the brakes, I saw the airspeed indicator jump from zero to eighty knots. Suddenly I spotted a warning light in the back seat as my rear canopy became unlocked and started to move just a little bit. Obviously, I transmitted this to Chopper immediately via our internal communications. We were already at rotation speed and lifting off at 180 knots. Climbing, accelerating, gear up, flaps up, and my canopy is shockingly unlocked! There was just enough space between the front sill of the rear canopy and the canopy rail that I could see that it was actually cracked open. The F-4 had an interesting linkage between the canopy and the ejection seat that I was strapped into, meaning that if the canopy came off, I would be in a *hot seat* and could be ejected at any moment. So we were trying to get rid of our fuel, dumping it and burning it down so we'd be able to come back and land. It was a perfect-weather day, but it seemed to take forever to bring our fuel load down low enough to land all while staying below 250 knots in case the canopy came off and I was to be inadvertently ejected.

We were flying over the Atlantic Ocean, east of Virginia Beach, for over thirty minutes with my canopy not moving but still *unlocked*! And there was a lot of discussion. There were squadron veterans and technicians on the radio with us from our ready room trying to decide whether it was better to come in and do a soft landing over a two-mile-long runway, or to take a field arrestment (landing), using the cables that lay across the runway while using our tail hook to do a shorter stop in less than one thousand feet. After deciding to make an arrested landing, we were finally on our approach. The canopy was still attached to the airplane as we were descending past 2,500 feet at 250 knots. Suddenly, I just heard this huge boom. It felt explosive, as if my canopy had been jettisoned. What actually happened was my canopy just ripped off due to the differential pressure between the cockpit and the atmosphere. I had lowered my seat as far as I could to stay out of the wind stream, and unbelievably we're flying around in an F-4 Phantom convertible. The back seat had no canopy. The front seat still had its canopy. And there was my humorist buddy, Chopper, piloting the Phantom with a moment of dead silence after my canopy came off. Chopper came up on the intercom.

"Are you still with me?" After a short pause, I said, "I'm still with you." The wind blast at 250 knots was eerily quiet even with my helmet and oxygen mask attached. I have to admit I was tempted to put my hand outside as if I were in my car with the window down but knew that would end badly. I stayed hunkered down but kept all the radio communications from the back seat as we were coming into land. We made an uneventful landing with the tailhook down, but now we had a different problem. With the F-4 Phantom stopped on the runway, sitting there, the engines still running, nobody wanted to get up over my seat because it was a hot seat that could potentially eject me at any moment. I sat in that seat for well over an hour, while the technicians came out and decided how best to extract me from the hot seat and cockpit. Eventually, all of that happened without incident. The airplane actually got fixed and flew again. But to have this unusual problem happen on one of my first operational flights was certainly my early introduction into how difficult it was to be in fighter aviation and how dangerous it could be. Frankly, after flying over 6,100 hours in various different types of fighters, this was one of the closest moments to actually ejecting I experienced. And it was at the *very* beginning of my flying career. My early lesson was not only that this is a dangerous business but also that good things still happen with smart, timely, and calculated decision-making.

Top Gun Training II: Key West to *Kitty Hawk*

Another major step in my training took place at Naval Air Station Key West, where my class of F-4 Phantom student aviators was introduced to air combat maneuvering training. We were graded on every single flight, and that's when my reputation was clearly molded. If you were in the top 5 percent of your class and you had very high grades, you *could* be awarded the Top Air Crew Award. The flight instructors had not awarded this honor for a couple of years. A fighter pilot named Scott "Lizard" Grant and I (we were often crewed together) received the Top Air Crew patch before we both went to our fleet squadron. This was the first recognition that separated me (and Lizard, as a crew) from the rest of our peers. These training events showcased how athletic you had to be in the cockpit along with mastering three-dimensional maneuvering and quick thinking. Many of these flights were one versus one, that is, against another jet, and eventually multijet fights with different simulated weapons. I fell in love with this part of the fighter mission and embraced its intensity and teamwork.

Right before I went to my fleet squadron, which was based in Japan, I had the chance to get my first carrier arrested landings on board the USS *Kitty Hawk* (CV-63), which was operating off the coast of San Diego, California.

The *Kitty Hawk* was a supercarrier (1961–2009) more than a thousand feet in length with a speed of over thirty-two knots, a crew of 5,600, and room on deck for up to ninety aircraft.

I was flying with a legendary fighter pilot named "Thunder Bud" Taylor, who would go on to be the commander of our sister squadron, the VF-151 Vigilantes. Flying with Bud was an amazing experience. He really showed me the ropes. We made ten daytime landings, known as "traps," and ten nighttime traps on the *Kitty Hawk* without flying over or skipping over the wires (known as a bolter) even once. Those twenty traps in September 1983 were the first landings of my eventual U.S. record-breaking two thousand traps reached in October 2012.

Bud saw something in me and did more than just let me experience my first traps. He taught me *and* mentored me.

When I eventually joined my fleet squadron, I was crewed up with my commanding officer, Commander "Willie" Williamson. I was the most junior aviator and naval flight officer in Fighter Squadron 161, the Rock Rivers. VF-161, flying the F-4S Phantom II along with eight other squadrons comprising fighters, attack aircraft, tankers, early warning, electronic attack, and helicopters, made up Carrier Air Wing Five. CVW-5 was permanently assigned to USS *Midway* (CV-41) stationed in Yokosuka, Japan. *Midway* was a World War II–built aircraft carrier and was well past her thirty-five years of service during my time aboard from 1983 to 1986. It was a unique period as the Cold War was still in effect and the most operational carrier and air wing were the oldest technology hardware in the fleet.

Willie was an exceptional fighter pilot. He had conducted over two hundred combat missions during the Vietnam War as well as being one of the best tailhook aviators I ever flew with. During my early time in VF-161, I flew nearly one hundred various missions with Willie, and he also proved to be an exceptional teacher, mentor, and boss. We experienced it all, from training flights, real-world intercept missions against Soviet large wing bombers, air-to-ground missions, air-to-air dogfighting, and landing on the pitching deck of the *Midway*, both day and night often with no land-based divert options, affectionally called "blue water" operations.

Top Gun Training III: "Night in the Barrel"

I was assigned to fly with a number of different pilots, and it was winter of 1984 that I was paired with Lieutenant Commander Vance "Steamer" Toalson, our operations officer. Earlier in his career, he had been a small boats operator working in a riverine squadron during the end of the Vietnam War. He had transitioned into being an experienced fighter pilot with VF-161. Steamer was known for being very capable in the airplane and was a superb tailhook pilot. We had flown together for well over a month and a half as we were starting to wind down our operations at the end of 1984.

A date forever etched in my memory was November 23, 1984. We were flying at night, operating in the Northern Sea of Japan (East Sea), and the sea state was actually pretty flat when we launched at 10 p.m. Other carriers operating in the same area were the USS *Enterprise* (CVN65) and the USS *Carl Vinson* (CVN70). It was unusual to be in three carrier operations, but they were far enough away that it was never going to be that much difference in terms of having a bigger deck than *Midway* to land as this real-life sea story unfolds.

After we catapulted from the USS *Midway*, there were twenty-five airplanes in the air. When we came back to make our night landing about an hour and a half later, the sea state had changed *dramatically*. The USS *Midway* was being bounced around at sea with high winds and massive waves. The ship moved as much as twenty to thirty feet in pitch of deck motion. Our hook to ramp clearance was only about nineteen feet, so with the deck moving that much, it was very dangerous. The *Midway*'s flight deck was forty feet above the water compared to sixty feet of today's Nimitz-class carriers, meaning that the blades of the ship's propellers were showing their tips in the pitching sea on some of the extreme deck excursions. We didn't even get a chance to put our wheels on the deck on our first approach. The deck was moving so much, the landing signal officers on the back end of the ship waved us off, and we went back around in the landing pattern. Meanwhile, the rest of the airborne package was slowly making its way to landing. Some pilots were having the same trouble landing as we were. We were blue water operations (meaning USS *Midway* was our only landing option), so our fuel state was managed to always have enough gas for at least two landing attempts, which meant that low-fuel-state aircraft would use airborne refueling from tanker-equipped jets assigned to *Midway*, flying directly overhead in a racetrack pattern.

After our third missed attempt at landing, we were directed to fly overhead the carrier to go up and refuel. Not only was this refueling at night, but it was pitch dark with cloud cover and vertigo-inducing conditions. We used our own refueling probe attached to the airplane, which plugged into a refueling basket and hose attached to either an A-7 Corsair or an A-6 Intruder. We took between 2,500 and 3,000 pounds of fuel pumped from the tanker to our jet and then came back down to 1,200 feet to make another attempt at landing. Most of the airplanes were landing by now, and we were coming down to make landing attempt number *four*, then number *five*. On landing attempt number six, we, for the first time in our many attempts, touched the deck. Every time we had tried to land up to this point, the deck would pitch up dramatically and we would be waved off. But on the sixth attempt, we landed well past the wires, throttles pushed to full military power, and we were airborne again. By now our fuel was low enough that we needed to go up overhead the carrier and refuel again. So we went through the same process again, only to come back down on landing attempt number seven and number eight with more wave-offs.

On landing attempt number nine we touched the deck again, but we landed past the wires. At this point, all aircraft have landed safely, with the exception of our F-4 Phantom and one last KA-6 tanker. We joined up to the tanker. The pilot of that tanker jet was Lieutenant "Hound Dog" McLean. Hound Dog would eventually become a Blue Angel pilot and a navy admiral. He had been paying close attention to how long we had been trying to land, and he gave us an extra thousand pounds of his own fuel, fuel that he needed to have multiple looks at the deck to land himself. And of course, as the final tanker pilot in blue water operations, if you can't land, there's no place else to go but eject. Well, as it worked out, Hound Dog went down, made his approach, and landed on his first attempt. We came down and did not even touch the deck on attempt number ten. Number eleven, we touched down but didn't catch the wires. Finally, as we were setting up for landing attempt number twelve, the captain of the USS *Midway*, H. P. Koehler, came on the radio to give us our options. We had been trying to land for two hours.

Captain Koehler's transmission was like hearing the voice of God. His voice was calm, cool, and exact: "Steamer, Slapshot, this is your night in the barrel. I know what your fuel state is. You've got enough fuel to come in and make one more attempt at landing. You have three choices. One. We can rig the barricade (a giant nylon web net) for you to fly into the net. Two. You can fly alongside the ship and make a controlled ejection, and we'll pluck you out of the water with helicopters. Three. You can try to make a normal landing, which you've been doing for a long time and have not been successful." What happened next was an amazing life lesson, because Steamer, who was much senior to me with all his experience, for the first time asked me what I thought we should do. I said, "Well, we don't want to fly into the net. That's pretty much an untested approach for this type of F-4 Phantom. Plus, it's harder to land in the net at night than it is to land in the wires, especially on a pitching deck." The water temperature was in the low forties, and our survivability on a dark night with heavy seas was not great. We had enough fuel for at least one more pass, so I didn't want us to eject right away.

I said, "Let's just make one more shot at the deck." So that's what we did. As we came in to make our attempt at landing, the deck pitched up more than we had seen it pitch up during any of the other attempts. Even at night, with the glow of the ship's aft drop lights, I saw the tips of the carrier's screws (propellers) churn out of the water. We were much higher above normal glide slope to make sure we cleared the ramp of the ship. We had made our plan and had every intention of just crash landing into the wires and hopefully pick a wire to stop. If we missed the wires, we would eject because we had not enough fuel for another approach. So as the nose came over and we descended to a one-thousand-feet-per-minute rate of descent (similar to jumping off a two-story building), the deck suddenly came down. We were coming down so fast in synch with the deck coming down, we intercepted and touched down hard as we caught the *last* wire, the number three wire, on board USS *Midway*. The airplane miraculously had no damage. It was the most intense and exciting moment of my flying career to that point. It was also my personal record for most approaches to land on an aircraft carrier, ever. When we got down into our ready room, it was like a scene from a movie, yes, even *Top Gun*. Everybody on the ship was excited. The whole ship's crew and every aviator were watching us and cheering for us on closed-circuit TV as the ultimate reality show was playing out live.

An Experience I Will Never Forget

We were met by the captain of the ship, the air wing commander, and our squadron mates. We got pulled into a little briefing room with our commanding officer of the squadron, Commander John "JP" Patton. He came up to Steamer and said, "So how was it up there? We want to know how you were doing." Steamer said, "Slapshot kept me going. He kept being my copilot and reminding me how well I was doing after every missed approach." It was at that very moment Steamer said to JP, "I'm going to recommend Ted Carter go to Top Gun." JP would eventually approve that recommendation, and my path to Top Gun was started.

Top Gun at the time was a very tough program to get into, especially from an overseas-based squadron. As some may recall in the original movie, it was stated that the top 1 percent of all naval aviators have the privilege to go to Top Gun. For Japan-based fighter squadrons, we got a slot for one pilot and naval flight officer to go to Top Gun every two years. So my timing was such that either this was my chance or I would simply miss out, as I would be transferring by the time the next quota came up.

Top Gun is a nickname for what began and is still known as the U.S. Navy Fighter Weapons School. It is a dedicated master's level U.S. Navy training program that teaches air combat, maneuvering tactics, and techniques to selected naval aviators and naval flight officers. Graduates return to their operating units as tactics instructors.

I was paired up with another navy lieutenant named Rory "Wiley" Banks. Rory and I started to fly together in preparation to go to Top Gun. After just a few months of flying together, we made the trip to Miramar Naval Air Station in San Diego, California. Our class at Top Gun started in February 1985 and would finish in late March 1985. This was the *final* class of all F-4 Phantoms consisting of eight fighter jets and four active-duty and four naval reserve squadrons, both U.S. Navy and Marine Corps. Being in the last all-Phantom class was noteworthy, as the very first classes at Top Gun featured the Phantom. It was dubbed the class of "the last of a legend, when speed was life." The reserve squadron pilots had a lot more flight time and a lot more experience than Rory and I did. I had over five hundred hours in the F-4, and Rory had about six hundred hours. Between the two of us, we had over three hundred carrier landings. To put it simply, we were very young for this graduate-level course. The Top Gun course in 1985 strictly focused on air-to-air missions. It was intense, as we flew twice a day, every day, and we had multiple lectures and courses mixed in daily. I was twenty-five years old, and Rory was twenty-eight.

Top Gun Process

We took a lot of classes and written tests. The preparation for classes and flights was exhaustive and time-consuming. There were so many experiences from that five weeks of training at Top Gun that I could make it a separate book.

I will recall two events that had significance in what Top Gun meant to me and why it was exciting to finish the program. In 1985 the navy had a classified program. It's now unclassified and, today, public knowledge. The program was called "Constant Peg," and it involved using our Top Gun instructor pilots to fly actual Soviet-era fighter jets that had been "procured" from a classified runway somewhere in the desert in Nevada. Our graduate training flight was one-versus-one air combat maneuvering (dogfight) against one of these airplanes. So we were directed to show up to a certain piece of sky over the desert of Nevada. This Soviet-era airplane, which was being flown by a Top Gun instructor, took off and met us to engage in a twenty-plus-mile head-to-head intercept. We did not know what type of airplane it was. The anticipation of fighting an actual Soviet-built MiG was incredible. This final test was based on everything we had been learning up to this point.

In our scenario, we were flying at fifteen thousand feet, speed of our choice. The bogey, or the unknown airplane, was to meet us at the same altitude, and we wouldn't know what that airplane was until we got visual contact. It was a blue-sky day with no clouds visible anywhere and bright sunshine, with well over forty miles of visibility. As we passed each other, separated by five hundred feet and well over one thousand knots of closure speed, we identified our bogey as a MiG-23. The MiG-23 was somewhat similar to the F-4 Phantom in terms of maneuverability. The jet had a swing wing and a big engine, and it was single-piloted with poor visibility from the cockpit. As we met each other at the merge, we immediately identified the jet but had to act almost instinctively to engage in the dogfight. We both thought, okay, we got a MiG-23. This is an airplane we know we can out-maneuver. We turned hard left with a little bit of nose down. Wiley pulled hard on the stick to make the best 6.5 g force turn he could put on the Phantom. What the MiG-23 pilot did next was a surprise, as he pulled the nose straight up and flew vertically into the sky. We had mistaken how fast he really was when he came into the merge. We pulled up into the vertical, but the MiG out-zoom-climbed us! And even though we thought we could beat this airplane, as he flew straight up into the sun, we lost sight of the MiG. Veteran, smart move by our instructor.

Our most humbling lesson was the most basic in a visual dogfight. "Lose sight, lose the fight." The whole fight lasted less than a minute because as the

Top Gun pilot came out of the sun, he rolled the jet over on its back, pointed its nose at us, and got a simulated kill on our airplane. We were a bit embarrassed in the debrief because we mis-assessed the speed at which the airplane came in and we learned that any airplane flown to the best of its ability can beat another airplane. It really does come down to the intelligence and skill of the air crew in determining winning versus losing. So it was a great lesson learned. It was one of the few times that we actually got shot during our entire Top Gun experience. And it was humbling to hold that lesson and put in our memory banks and never forget it. The last story I would like to share was the myth of a Top Gun trophy. There is really no such thing. But the top air crew in the class was tasked to brief, plan, and lead, as well as debrief, the final Top Gun flying event, a major complex simulated strike evolution. This mission involved over sixty airplanes, half of which were being flown by Top Gun pilots as enemy opposition.

Rory and I planned the mission, but I was privileged to do the brief and debrief in front of seventy-five aviators. It was a complex flight. Of course, there was a box score for how many simulated kills were made on each side, and eventually an assessment of mission success and a determination of who actually won. It was the most complex set of tactics utilizing the culmination of all five weeks of training at Top Gun. We flew it over a land range in the high desert. The mountainous terrain made it difficult for us to use our radars compared to being over the water. In the air-to-air fight, and in the air-to-ground fight, we were successful. Our strike package made it to the target and released their bombs, completing their mission. We had more than a three-to-one kill ratio of enemy aircraft to friendly fighters. So, it was evaluated as a success. The next day we received our Top Gun certificates and our Top Gun patches; I wore my patch for the rest of my flying career.

I felt immense pride and a sense of belonging in this elite field of Top Gun graduates. We immediately returned to our fighter squadrons. Rory Banks and I went back to the USS *Midway*, where we continued to fly together. But now we had a different role. Now we were expected to go back and be instructors in our squadrons to take the latest tactics, latest understanding of missile technology, and the most recent understanding of the Soviet threat in the air-to-air arena.

A Teacher for Life

The important part of this Top Gun experience for me was that it established me as a teacher for life. I never stopped being a teacher, whether I was assigned instructor duty or operational command. I enjoyed what it meant to be in that arena as a fighter aviator. When I eventually left USS *Midway* and VF-161 in 1986, I got orders to return to NAS Miramar. I was to be an F-14 Tomcat instructor. With no previous time in the Tomcat, I spent six months learning every aspect of the jet to become an instructor. I stayed as a flight instructor in the F-14 Tomcat for almost four years after Top Gun. I was in Fighter Squadron 124, the Gunfighters, teaching air-to-air tactics, weapons, and basic F-14 familiarization and even had two years as an air show performer.

Top Gun, as much as it was advertised about being the best of the best, was really about understanding teaching and learning and what it means to be at the top of your game, to be able to impart that knowledge onto others, to get them to experience that elite level so they can continue to grow and learn. I had over 350 carrier landings coming off the *Midway*, with over one thousand hours in the F-4 Phantom. I spent a lot of time in the back seat with some very young pilots and some experienced pilots. Over the course of those four years, I went to every aircraft carrier on the West Coast with *thirty-two different pilots*. Some of those pilots had failed in their earlier attempts to get qualified and fly the F-14 Tomcat, so I was often their instructor on their second attempt to qualify. I learned my own skill set to get the best out of new fighter pilots by keeping them calm and teaching them the sense of teamwork. This approach worked well. In 1987 I was selected as the F-14 Tomcat flight instructor of the year. And the following year I was selected as naval aviation's junior tailhooker of the year because I had almost nine hundred carrier landings as a young lieutenant, the most in the entire fleet. I had made the reputation of being a top flight instructor over those four years, especially teaching carrier operations. My biggest motivation after being a Top Gun graduate as well as an F-14 Tomcat instructor was just how much I loved seeing that lightbulb turn on for a young naval aviator as they were going through that training phase and then to see them be successful in the fleet.

And that's why my Top Gun experience stayed with me. It stayed with me while I was flying combat missions all the way until I had squadron command. It stayed with me while I was rebuilding a nuclear-powered aircraft carrier. It stayed with me while I was taking ships to sea. It stayed with me while I was the president of the Naval War College, the superintendent of the Naval Academy, and yes, I even brought it with me to Nebraska and Ohio when I became the president of the University of Nebraska system and Ohio State University.

As I reflect on my career, from my Top Gun training and my time as an instructor to being a commanding officer of ships, squadrons, and even a fleet of over twenty ships and thousands of service men and women, I realize how much I enjoy teaching, mentoring, and empowering others to be successful.

Leadership is fulfilling but demanding—mentally, physically, and emotionally. To be in that top 1 percent to 5 percent of work, school, or sports requires not only discipline and mental skills but also a determination to stay focused during every interaction with anyone and everyone.

Mental Skills

For an elite aviator, visualization is critical and does not just mean great twenty-twenty eyesight. The ability to analyze and anticipate where your aircraft is, where it's going, and where it needs to be is often the difference between losing versus winning and, in some cases, survival.

Each of the mental skills identified in the following chapters were critical to my success: Sleep, relaxation, and instant relaxation are necessary in times of crisis—whether you are in training or are being shot at with surface-to-air missiles (SAMs). I learned these skills, which allowed me to mentally slow down in real time to make split-second decisions for survival and mission success.

The ability to compartmentalize, blocking out life's stressors and focus, is a critical skill for winning.

Preflight focus and energy-enhancing sleep are essential particularly for high performance and long flights. One of the scenes in *Top Gun: Maverick* was the performance of a tactic called the "consecutive miracles." The mission for Tom Cruise, the Top Gun instructor, and his training pilots involved a terrifyingly low-level, high-speed flight to avoid radar locking of SAMs and then a maneuver to send two laser-guided weapons to penetrate and blow up a target going down a three-square-meter ventilation shaft into a potential nuclear power plant.

In real life I flew a mission into Iraq in 1999 with two F-14A Tomcats using the consecutive miracle tactic. The scenario was not exactly the same as the movie (no low-level ingress), but the tactic of using precision targeting to send two laser-guided bombs into a three-square-meter vent line was based on a real tactic and was depicted accurately in the *Top Gun: Maverick* movie.

In my case, I was the commanding officer of Fighter Squadron 14, the Tophatters. I was allowed to handpick the aircrew for the mission (similar to the movie), and it did involve enemy fire as we flew to a release point to send two large, two-thousand-plus-pound laser-guided bombs into a heavily fortified, deeply buried command and control bunker just outside Baghdad. We were successful in that mission because of not only all the tactics and procedures learned at Top Gun but also the mental skills developed in combat over the years. Visualization and staying relaxed (prior to and during the mission) were as important to mission success as the detailed planning and flying execution.

PART 2

TOP GUN PERFORMANCE ACROSS LIFE STAGES

.

3

Top Gun Performance—School and Sports

Good leaders possess self-awareness, garner credibility, focus on
relationship building, have a bias for action, exhibit humility,
empower others, stay authentic, present themselves as constant
and consistent, become role models, and are fully present.

—BRIAN TRACY

Youth

I, Ted Carter, grew up in a small town, Burrillville, Rhode Island (population,
seventeen thousand). I was the oldest of three children. Burrillville was a one-
high-school town, about two hundred young men and women being in my
high school class. The town was small enough that my mother, as an English
teacher, taught me three out of my four years in high school English. I was fortunate to have her, as she was not only a terrific teacher but an incredible role
model. While I was growing up, both my parents believed in sports. They also
believed in being involved in other things, and I was given lots of opportunities.

I was given an opportunity to do everything from playing musical instruments to playing sports to participating in academic competitions.

I played woodwind instruments, the clarinet and saxophone. I played in the
school band and was even in the marching band. Much to the consternation
of my parents I was in my own band with some friends, and we wrote some
of our own music. I was even offered a full-ride scholarship to the Berklee
College of Music in Boston.

I participated in sports like ice hockey, basketball, track and field, baseball,
and soccer from the age of six all the way through high school and college.
I was involved in all those sports at varying levels, from Little League up to
Babe Ruth Leagues in baseball. I played in many hockey leagues all over New
England and even played in Canada when I was thirteen.

The passion for hockey runs deep in Burrillville—the town had a junior hockey league for seventy years.

My parents also believed strongly in public education. I was fortunate to attend a good public high school and was well prepared by the time I entered ninth grade, coming out of Burrillville Junior High School. I also got straight A's all the way through my four years of high school; I ended up graduating third in my class.

My work ethic, moral development, and desire to learn were shaped by supportive parents and a busy but happy childhood.

I applied to quite a few different undergraduate schools, from Harvard to Brown University and a lot of other high-profile schools. But in my sophomore year in high school I met a young man named Matt Elias, who was from Smithfield, Rhode Island, and was a sophomore at the U.S. Naval Academy. He came to my high school during Thanksgiving of 1975 and inspired me to look into going to the U.S. Naval Academy. The application to Annapolis was a long, drawn-out process. It was somewhat confusing to both me and my parents, but we navigated it. I took The Rhode Island civil service exam and did well enough to be the seventh alternate to get into the Naval Academy under Senator Claiborne Pell. I thought that was a little too low on the alternate list with one or two selectees, so I kind of gave up on the dream of maybe going to sea or being a naval aviator.

Something special happened in my senior year, however, thanks to the inspirational work of my high school biology teacher, Mr. Frank Hauser. I had stayed with a science project that I started as a freshman. I eventually took this project to the Rhode Island state level, where I won the top prize in the spring of 1977. I then went on to an international science fair where I won two significant prizes, one in biochemistry and the other in oceanography. My science project focused on water pollution in Rhode Island's ponds and wells, using water daphnia (water fleas) as natural pollutant indicators.

The prize in oceanography was sponsored by the U.S. Naval Institute. Shortly after the competition, on April 15, 1977, I was notified of my appointment and was accepted to the Naval Academy. That same day, I was accepted to Brown University. Brown had been my primary plan as a prestigious Ivy League school with an acceptance rate of 5 percent and requiring a 4.08 GPA or higher. After long discussions with my parents, I decided to go to the Naval Academy. My parents were influential in that decision. We didn't have many military connections in our background, certainly nobody who had served in the U.S. Navy. It was a risk to say the least, but my parents believed I could make it work.

The Naval Academy had an acceptance rate of 8 percent with a dropout rate of 35 percent in 1977. When I showed up there in July of that summer, I was young and naïve. I had traveled out of the state only twice, once to play hockey in Canada and the other time to go to the international science fair in Cleveland, Ohio. But I had a good work ethic. I knew I wanted to play sports, and I was fortunate that I was able to make the ice hockey team at Navy with only three freshmen on the roster.

Even though playing hockey and taking classes were a big workload, my discipline and past training got me through the grueling demands of being a midshipman.

Classes were much more difficult than anything I had experienced in high school. It was a tough, sometimes frustrating, but fantastic experience. I was also fortunate to have been so well-rounded in high school. I was on the school newspaper staff, the yearbook staff, and in many other clubs in high school. So I joined the magazine staff at the U.S. Naval Academy.

The *LOG Magazine* of the Naval Academy dated back to the early 1900s and was an organization of midshipmen who published a humorous periodical for the enjoyment of the brigade. It was something of a sports and humor magazine and an outlet for creativity, artistic ability, and comedic talent. I stayed with that, actually becoming the editor in chief my junior and senior years—while I was still playing ice hockey and while I began dating my future wife, Lynda.

Lynda and I met during my sophomore year, in January 1979. I was carrying a full academic load as an oceanography major, playing hockey, and being managing editor of the *LOG*.

My hockey experience gave me my eventual naval aviator call sign of "Slapshot," but also, and more important, it led to my meeting Lynda. She was a student at the University of Maryland and was attending our first "date" hockey game when I broke out of sophomore slump, scoring two short-handed goals in a 4–2 victory against Duquesne. We dated the remaining two and a half years I was at Navy and were engaged to be married shortly after I graduated.

I hate admitting that my grades at the Naval Academy were not as good as they could have been. I was never in any kind of academic trouble, but because I was doing all these other activities (my choice), it was really a time management challenge. That challenge formed the basis of my behavior and my personality. I was able to do multiple things at the same time, trying to keep myself totally engaged while understanding and working with different people and different backgrounds. Perhaps this is where I learned my passion for team building. I was deeply honored to receive the big "C" on my ice hockey jersey, which signaled that I had been selected by my teammates to be team captain. This historic tradition of hockey is considered its highest honor, and I wore the patch proudly.

I was so fortunate to have grown up in a small town. Burrillville, founded in the early 1800s as a textile and mill town, was older than the Naval Academy itself, established in 1845. I was the first Burrillville High School graduate to ever attend the U.S. Naval Academy, but I had no idea until I was almost ready to graduate.

In 2023 I was honored to have the 1970s-era high school gym in Burrillville rededicated to me and named the Vice Admiral Walter "Ted" Carter Gymnasium. The event, held in front of so many family and friends, as well as the entire senior class of Burrillville, was the most humbling of my career. I will never forget where I came from.

I was mostly driven and motivated by the gifts that my parents gave me: the ability to study, that is, get the most out of study hours, and the ability to do so many other things as well, such as play sports, write, and play musical instruments.

So as I look back on my Naval Academy time and see how young I was, I wonder what made me successful and what drove me to be successful. The truth is, I wasn't sure what I wanted to do in the navy. From the day I entered the academy, I was enamored with the idea of getting to fly fighter jets. But I also had this sense that because I'm in the navy, I should go to sea and be on ships, maybe drive ships. So I had this idea that maybe I'll be able to do more than one thing, similar to what I had been doing in high school. That would eventually prove to be true as I commanded squadrons, ships, and a nuclear-powered aircraft carrier.

As I reflect, I am thankful for my teachers in high school. But the most important thing that I got out of my high school experience was a great foundation in math and science. And of course I was driven pretty hard by my own mother in study skills, discipline, writing critically, and reading comprehension.

I got all that in a public high school.

The Naval Academy experience took me to another level. The math courses were very, very difficult. The English courses required a lot of reading. I used my time management skills to make sure that my technical courses were the ones that I got the A's in. And those would set me up later down the road. Little did I know that those A's in physics and math were what allowed me to be successful in the navy's nuclear-power school after I commanded a fighter squadron—and that would eventually lead to an aircraft carrier command. Unlike my academic performance at USNA, I completely immersed myself in the rigorous year-and-a-half-long nuclear power program. It was the hardest I had ever worked, achieving exceptional grades at the age of forty and embarking on a twelve-year run as a nuclear engineer.

Preparing Leaders

I am blessed to have had special teachers and mentors in my career. A seed was planted. I would eventually become an educator and a mentor myself.

I've given a lot of speeches in my career. My favorite was to the incoming class (called "plebes") of 2023 at the Naval Academy. On their induction day in late June 2019, I gave my last speech as superintendent of the Naval Academy, a tour that lasted five years. I prided myself over the years on delivering keynote speeches from memory and from my heart. I learned this skill at Top Gun and still use it today.

The following is an excerpt, the final words of that speech. The audience was 1,200 plebes and five thousand family members of those plebes.

If you do these two things you will make it through the forty-two days of training and be here to greet your parents for Plebe Parents Weekend in early August.

The first thing is really easy. Do what you're told. Do what you're told.

The second one is going to be harder for you, because you're going to make some mistakes. Some of you have never made a mistake in your young lives. You've been that good. You've been that accomplished. But you will fail. And some of you are going to want to give up. But the second thing you have to do every single day is give your best. You do those two things, do what you're told and give it your best. And this plebe summer experience will work out just fine.

Now of course, your training starts really right now. And part of your training as a soon-to-be Naval Academy plebe is to understand the very history of who we are, what we represent, what our values are. I will tell you just a very short story as you can begin to know some of the most famous naval sayings that you will ever, ever hear. This one dates back to August 5, 1864, near the tail end of the Civil War.

The battle to capture Atlanta was centered around one thing—to prevent the waterway of the Confederate navy to get into Mobile, Alabama, and resupply the Confederate forces. Rear Admiral David Glasgow Farragut was in charge of the large Union navy. He brought fifteen ships including four ironclads to Mobile Bay at 5:30 a.m. A quick-moving tide was moving through the harbor. He sent his ironclads in first, with the rest of his ships, two columns lashed together. He sat in his flagship, the USS *Hartford*. Toward the rear, second in the line, the USS *Tecumseh*, an ironclad with 114 souls, went through the harbor, staying away from the guns of Fort Morgan. A mine, commonly known as a torpedo in those days, exploded under the ship, sending the bow of the ship shot straight up, and it sank like an arrow coming off of an archer's bow. All 114 souls were lost at sea.

The lead captain on the USS *Brooklyn*, another ironclad, was Captain Alden, who stopped the formation and reversed his engines. In the smoke of combat, Admiral Farragut could not see the battlefield of the Gulf of Mobile Bay. He climbed the main mast. He strapped himself to the rigging so he could see the battle.

He called for a right full rudder of the USS *Hartford*. He quickly sailed up next to the lead ship and yelled at Captain Alden, "Damn those torpedoes. Full speed ahead."

Full speed ahead indeed. Class of 2023, your charge is now to go full speed ahead. As we think about where you are right now, we think about some of the greatest naval heroes that have really depicted the energy and the personality of our United States Navy. I can think of no greater naval hero than John Paul Jones, buried right here in our Naval Academy crypt. John Paul Jones was a diminutive character, only five feet six inches, an immigrant from Scotland.

He never lost a battle at sea. He was known for saying, "I have not yet begun to fight. I wish to have no connection with any ship that does not sail fast while I intend to go in harm's way." But on this day, as you are moments away from taking an oath, an oath not to a person but to an ideal, to promote and protect freedom and democracy and take an oath to our constitution, John Paul Jones, in 1777, 242 years ago, was recruiting young men to go into combat, combat that was not very attractive for a lot of new Americans.

These words from 1777 ring just as true today as they did then. These are the words of John Paul Jones . . .

"Sign on. Come sail with me. The stature of our homeland is no more than the measure of ourselves. Our job is to keep her free. Our will is to keep the torch of freedom burning for all. To the solemn purpose, we call on the young, the brave, the strong, and the free. Heed my call. Come to the sea. Come sail with me."

Class of 2023, sail on.

Congratulations. May God bless all of you, the class of 2023, your parents, your loved ones, our United States Naval Academy, our Navy Marine Corps team, and our United States of America. Thank you all. Go Navy.

The class of 2023 would go on to break records at the Naval Academy. In almost every measure from sports, academics, military bearing, and graduation rates, I was proud to have been their superintendent on induction day.

In August 2022 I had the honor of being named a Distinguished Graduate of the U.S. Naval Academy. It is Navy's highest award and a lifetime achievement honoring me, my family, and all those teammates with whom I served.

As wonderful as that day was, the biggest memory was addressing the entire 4,400 members of the brigade of midshipmen. The members of the class of 2023 were just beginning their senior year, and it was fitting that I spoke to them both on induction day and now as seniors. In my final comments, I spoke to service, and even though my days at sea were well behind me, it was now their turn to perform and inspire others to do as Captain John Paul Jones implored: "Come to the sea, come sail with me."

4

Top Gun Performance—Work

The very essence of leadership is that you have to have a vision.
It's got to be a vision you articulate clearly and forcefully on
every occasion. You can't blow an uncertain trumpet.
—REVEREND THEODORE HESBURGH (1917–2015)

The ultimate measure of a person is not where one stands in moments of
comfort and convenience, but where one stands in time of challenge.
—MARTIN LUTHER KING JR.

My childhood idol was Canadian hockey player Wayne Gretzky. He played twenty seasons in the National Hockey League and became known as "the Great One." Many sportswriters called him the greatest hockey player ever. He was a gifted athlete at only six feet and 185 pounds. His greatest attribute was his mental game. He played hard and smart.

Gretzky's famous quotation is one that I have adopted, especially when it comes to performance in school, sports, and work. "A good hockey player plays where the puck is. A great hockey player plays where the puck is going to be." This philosophy and mantra in one has guided me and prepared me to perform at my best for each stage in my career. My mentors have always encouraged me to stay ahead of the curve—preparing me to be ready for the next challenge in my career.

Career Stage I

My career as an aviator after Top Gun school in 1985 required that 70 percent of my time be spent at sea. This obligation posed some unique challenges for my relationships with family and friends.

Team Carter, consisting of my supportive wife and two kids, made this process possible. At last count, our family has moved twenty-eight times during my career. Being successful in any career requires dedication and discipline as well as support from one's family, for which I am forever grateful.

I was flying the F-4 Phantom and the F-14 Tomcat when I was first deployed around the globe. It was an honor to be able to land on nineteen different aircraft carriers, including all ten of the Nimitz-class carriers.

I was then assigned to command Fighter Squadron 14, the Tophatters.

The next promotion was as the executive officer (second in command) of the USS *Harry S. Truman* (CVN 75), an aircraft carrier with 5,500 service men and women. It was a special experience for me to be appointed as the captain of both a combat replenishment ship and a nuclear-powered aircraft carrier, USS *Camden* (AOE 2) and USS *Carl Vinson* (CVN 70). It was a special thrill to command the USS *Enterprise* carrier strike group during its final combat deployment after fifty-one years as the largest ship in the U.S. Navy.

During all of these flying and command positions, my passion was flying and leading other aviators on 125 combat missions in support of joint operations in Bosnia, Kosovo, Kuwait, Iraq, and Afghanistan. I was able to accumulate 6,150 flight hours during my career and safely completed 2,016 carrier arrested landings, the record among all active and retired U.S. Naval aviation designators. Amazingly, I never ejected from any aircraft in my thirty-eight-year career.

My leadership skills were tested when leading over twenty ships at sea (to include two aircraft carriers) in the Middle East at a time involving over fifteen thousand service men and women, especially when we were patrolling the waters of the Strait of Hormuz for counterpiracy interdiction. You can imagine the challenges of commanding this many young individuals under extraordinary circumstances involving billions of dollars of highly technical equipment and the constant strain of high performance without loss of life.

The core moral values of my parents and numerous mentors guided me along a path of performance that resulted in many successes. I was able to achieve success only due to building amazing high-performance teams and a resulting culture of team unity. Good things happen when a leader focuses on building morale and reinforcing exceptional performance.

Of all the awards and decorations I have received, three stand out in my career.

The Distinguished Flying Cross with combat distinction—a very high honor for valor, awarded for aerial achievement in combat. I received this decoration for actions as mission commander and strike lead in an F-14A Tomcat on April 6, 1999. The mission was the first into Kosovo during Operation Allied Force and was successful under intense enemy fire.

The U.S. Navy League's John Paul Jones Award for inspirational leadership—one of the highest awards in the navy.

The James Bond Stockdale Leadership Award—the highest peer-based award in the navy. Stockdale was a Naval Academy graduate in 1946 and was to become one of the most decorated pilots in the navy for his service in Vietnam. He was shot down and spent seven years in an unimaginable prison with torture and solitary confinement. Stockdale refused to admit the United States was engaging in criminal behavior against the Vietnamese people. Upon his release he received the Medal of Honor (highest honor in the nation) and went on to become president of the Naval War College, president of Citadel University, and a senior research fellow at Stanford. His career path inspired me to progress to a university leadership position after thirty-eight years in the military. Admiral Stockdale and his wife, Sybil, presented me this award in person at the Pentagon. It was the last time he and his wife would be present together for this honor.

Career Stage II

My leadership duties significantly changed when I was assigned to shore duty and eventually becoming commander of the Joint Enabling Capabilities and lead of the transition planning team for the Joint Forces Command. That planning effort involved closing one of ten U.S. combatant commands, a historic first. We got it done in less than eight months.

My preparation for an academic assignment included my focus on the number one problem in universities—mental health. I was selected and honored to lead Task Force RESILIENT (a study in suicide-related behaviors). Task Force RESILIENT is a term that can refer to different initiatives or programs that aim to promote resilience among different groups of people, such as soldiers, first responders, or communities. Resilience is the ability to cope with adversity and adapt to change, recover, learn, and grow after setbacks.

My new assignment allowed me to shift from the mental and physical aspects of individuals between ages eighteen and thirty (the core ages of service men and women in the navy) to the emotional personality due to soaring rates of mental illness at 40 percent in this age group.

Also, I was tabbed in 2013 to establish the 21st Century Sailor Office as its first director, and this model is still in use to today.

All of these experiences prepared me for an academic leadership role, even though I had no advanced terminal degree (i.e., a PhD). I was asked to prepare a paper for presentation for the position of president of the U.S. Naval War College (NWC).

I was surprised at the offer, but I was told by senior leadership that they wanted someone with operational experience as opposed to a purely academic background—a shift at the NWC. The chief of naval operations, Admiral Jonathan Greenert, gave me a homework assignment by asking me to describe how I would lead the Naval War College if I were selected as president. This was an incredible opportunity for me to take my operational experience from Top Gun to task force commander in order to command the oldest war college of its kind in the world and modernize the U.S. Naval War College.

I submitted the following document, and perhaps it provides some insight into the new role of leadership training that I would be privileged to create, to direct, and have a lasting impact on.

January 1, 2013

MEMORANDUM FOR THE CHIEF OF NAVAL OPERATIONS

SUBJECT: U.S. Naval War College (NWC)—The Way Ahead

The U.S. Naval War College has been the preeminent academic institution for the study of the complexities of war and conflict since 1884, when it was founded by RADM Stephen B. Luce. It is the oldest institute of its kind for higher learning among the four services and has enjoyed an unmatched rich history of success. If selected to lead the NWC, my vision would be to elevate the College to a new level of excellence by providing leaders and thinkers to contribute directly to the success of the Navy and our Nation in this new century. My thoughts for the way ahead are based upon my experience with existing military organizations and my understanding of today's role of the NWC.

When the NWC was founded, its function was for the education of experienced officers in advanced strategy, tactics, and logistics. It quickly developed into a de facto planning staff contributing significantly to the war effort by studying conflict with Spain over Cuba in 1896. Years later, following the efforts of WWI, our Nation faced a serious economic crisis, reduced spending in military resources and a reassessment of national strategy. It was this period during the interwar years in the late 20's and 30's when the NWC applied critical and strategic thinking to evolve ideas and concepts to prepare our leaders for conflict. Innovative thinking led to advancements in Naval aviation, submarine tactics, amphibious warfare, and logistics operations in order to sustain our forces across the world's oceans.

There is no question that the NWC and our Navy had a more direct influence over how it was used in war at the turn of our previous century; however, I believe we are in a similar period of time today, needing to build further on the success of the NWC Planner Curriculum, and utilizing our intellectual capital to present a range of solutions for our Fleet Commanders and Combatant Commanders.

As I look at the current list of missions at the NWC, they serve to build on the legacy of yesterday's NWC while sustaining momentum into many new efforts to set the conditions for a successful tomorrow. Given the multitude of other educational institutions across the joint force as well as the various organizations tasked with looking to the future, the NWC mission should refocus on two measurable, solution-oriented tasks in order to elevate itself to a new level as the premier academic center for how we fight in our Navy and Armed Forces.

Mission One: Educate Leaders

Educate today's leaders for tomorrow through professional military academics focusing on military strategy and policy, leadership, and warfighting. Return these leaders to the Fleet and apply their critical thinking skills to plan and execute operations successfully in peacetime and, when required, in crisis and conflict.

Mission Two: Shape the Future Navy

Lead and collaborate in war gaming, simulations, and research as well as sea power symposium efforts across the Fleet, joint and international communities of interest to bring innovative solutions to Fleet Commanders for near (<5 years), mid (5–10 years), and far (>10 years) term problems in order to shape and influence the Fleet of the future to deter aggression and win in crisis and conflict.

There are numerous subtasks that reside inside these mission priorities. However, I believe we need to look at the level of effort expended on activities in order to stay focused on delivering educated leaders and solutions for our Fleet Commanders.

If selected as the NWC President, I would commit to a series of focused achievable goals.

1. As President, I would expand the "reach" of the College. There are many products that have been produced by the College but where do those products go? Leading and collaborating with other Navy, Joint, and Coalition military centers of excellence, I would ensure that the research of the Strategic Studies Group (SSG), War Gaming products of students and faculty are coordinated and ultimately serve the Navy Warfighter. These organizations include but are not limited to the Naval Postgraduate School (NPS), Navy Warfare Development Center (NWDC), Office of Naval Research (ONR), Air Land Sea Application (ALSA) Center, Allied Command Transformation Innovation Directorate, and organizations such as the U.S. Naval Institute to publish potential outcomes through Proceedings Magazine.

All of these organizations along with the other Service and Joint War Colleges share similar missions and tasks to educate leaders and shape future forces. Without an understanding of what each organization is doing and what ultimately happens to products developed, we risk duplication of effort and ineffectiveness in applying the right resources to achieve the right solutions for our Warfighters.

We would continue to collaborate with International Navies but would focus on achievable outcomes though these symposiums.

Agreements to how we operate and establish basic command and control in forming a Joint and Combined Maritime Task Force to respond to natural disasters is a good example of achievable solutions from these forums.

2. As President, I would commit to addressing key issues for the Fleet. Your recent "Sailing Directions" serve us well in keeping us focused on warfighting first, operating forward, and remaining ready. Understanding our environment in a complex and dynamically changing world requires us to remain flexible but looking forward to ultimately stay the course for our sailing priorities. Your recent emphasis on payloads over platforms, the new cyber/electronic warfare dimension, and our shift to the Pacific Theater are areas of particular interest for our NWC to develop. The students at the NWC would address these (as opposed to a focus on faculty writings) future issues through their research, participation in war gaming, and writing in order to bring their expertise and talent back to the Fleet.

3. As President, I would commit to engaging myself personally in a candid and frank leadership seminar with every level of leader from Department Heads to future Unit Commanders and Senior Enlisted Chief Petty Officers. I believe I can make a positive difference in discussing real Fleet leadership challenges to be successful at sea, in combat, or in the shipyard.

4. As President, I would commit to giving the best minds named to attend the NWC what they need to do their best thinking, research, and writing.

5. As President, I will seek commitment from our Navy to nominate only the very best to attend the NWC in order to produce the top-notch thinking, research, and writing to further advance our Navy's core definition of "How we fight."

The success and enviable history of the NWC is inspiring. Its legacy of relevance to our Navy is without peer. If selected to lead the NWC, I will commit to foster and maintain an environment for our "best and brightest." Together, we will work to educate our leaders, return them to the Fleet, and shape the Navy of the future to promote and protect our National maritime interests.

> Walter "Ted" Carter
> Rear Admiral, USN
> CCSG-12

I was selected as the fifty-fourth president of the Naval War College, perhaps due to this new vision for which direction the NWC should take.

All successful leaders should frequently pause and ask themselves if their work is making a difference. Does my work fulfill my sense of purpose, and did I make a difference?

During this year-and-a-half effort, I was honored to establish the Naval Leadership and Ethics Center. A blueprint for how we should conduct our behavior, the center continues to shape our top leaders in the U.S. Navy for decades to come.

Career Stage III: Annapolis—Back to Where It All Started

In 2014 I was selected as the sixty-second superintendent of the U.S. Naval Academy—my dream job. The Naval Academy was established in 1845 and is situated in Annapolis, Maryland, thirty miles south of Baltimore, Maryland, and thirty miles east of Washington DC.

The academy educates midshipmen for service in the officer corps of the U.S. Navy and the U.S. Marine Corps.

The academy's motto is "Ex scientia tridens," Latin for "Through Knowledge, Sea Power!" Its academic staff consists of six hundred faculty, who teach 4,500 midshipmen. Tuition is free in exchange for a minimum of five years active-duty service. Some 1,200 plebes enter each year with over 1,000 graduating after their four years of training.

Graduates are commissioned as ensigns in the U.S. Navy or as second lieutenants in the U.S. Marine Corps. Midshipmen are required to adhere to the academy's HONOR CONCEPT.

The curriculum consists of core classes plus twenty-five major fields of study within three divisions:

Division 1—Engineering and Weapons,
Division 2—Math and Science, and
Division 3—Humanities and Social Science.

Moral and ethical development is fundamental to all aspects of the Naval Academy. Graduates include astronauts, Rhodes scholars, Heisman Trophy winners, and a U.S. president.

I was asked to serve as superintendent for five years—the longest continuously serving leader of the academy since the Civil War.

I was blessed with a talented academic team whereby we achieved repeated number one national rankings and new records in student success. We even beat our rival, Army West Point, fourteen years in a row in the annual Army-Navy football game.

My thirty-eight years in the military prepared me to be a Top Gun performer in leadership and "mental skills development," which we hope to share with others—the purpose of this book.

Career Stage IV: Civilian Academia

After a purpose-driven career in the military with unimaginable opportunities at the highest level, I was not looking at a career in academics. It was only after a search firm reached out to me to apply for the University of Nebraska's presidency that I considered such a prestigious position. After reading the job description, my wife, Lynda, said, "That's you, Ted. They are describing what you do best, and they have a hockey team in Omaha also."

After being selected as the priority candidate I went through a series of interviews over weeks traveling throughout the state. I thoroughly enjoyed the process. It was a natural fit for our family. The Nebraska University has fifty thousand students, sixteen thousand staff, and a $3 billion budget.

There was certainly a shift in focus, from an internal focus at the Naval Academy to an external focus on fundraising, working with the state legislature and the governor's office for funding priorities, and attending to Big Ten academics and sports.

During the four years I spent at the University of Nebraska, I (along with every other university and college president in the country) was tested by the impact of COVID challenges. Many top universities closed school except for online classes.

Bold leadership training kicked in, and we stayed open with an increase of 2 percent in enrollment during 2020. To boost enrollment we created a program called Nebraska Promise. This tuition break was to attract middle- and lower-income students. Any Nebraska family with an adjusted gross income of $65,000 or less received free tuition. If they lived at home, they could attend school free, a great opportunity for first-generation students.

We achieved improved academic accreditation and kept enrollment high with only a slight drop while raising the bar on research dollars.

Our experience with building teams, hiring exceptional talent, developing relationships with donors, obtaining funding from the state, and expanding internships and scholarships put us on a path to significantly improving our national rankings.

Our plan was to stay at Nebraska until retirement. We were happy and enjoyed all that Nebraska had to offer.

Higher education is extremely challenging today in a far different way than combat missions.

In the Big Ten, with eighteen schools, there were eight new presidents, some positions had no candidates apply for the top positions, and some leaders left after only two years. Perhaps it's the new normal. The average job duration for a president at a Power 5 conference school is 4.2 years, the same as Fortune 500 CEOs, head football coaches in the NFL, and football coaches at elite universities.

The challenge of leadership is in holding people accountable, something that was essential in the military. In higher education and in the business world, holding others accountable often results in resistance.

Change is hard, particularly in today's environment of competing political views, budget restraints, and questioning the value of a college degree.

I received many inquiries from some of the most prestigious schools in the country but turned them down. It was only after numerous conversations and a heavy recruiting effort that I accepted my latest leadership challenge.

In 2024 Lynda and I moved to Columbus, Ohio, and I assumed the position as the seventeenth president of the Ohio State University. The challenges are mostly the same at all major universities, but the timing and fit seemed to best meet my skill set and ability to serve in the capacity of meeting Ohio State's needs.

Perhaps one obvious difference between Nebraska and Ohio State is the scale of operation at the latter: twice as large in students, faculty, and staff and three times the operating budget, at $9 billion. It has the third-largest campus in the country and is at the top of the rankings in academics, research, and athletics.

There is no escaping my passion for teaching, leading, and mentoring particularly young students—from fighter pilots to MDs and PhDs. I think of the impact that these young leaders will make on the world and know that we did all we could to make it a better place, just like my teacher-mother taught me and my siblings.

There is nothing more satisfying in life than to have the privilege and opportunity to make a positive difference and lifelong opportunities for students.

PART 3

TOP GUN PERFORMANCE SKILLS

5

Performance Relaxation

We hate to lose more than we love to win. And we really, really love to win!
To perform at an exceptional level at everything in life! For our entire life!

—TED CARTER AND JACK STARK

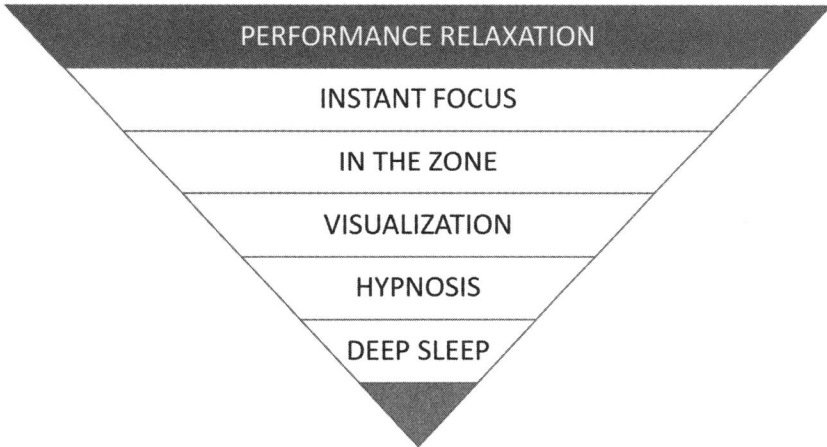

PERFORMANCE RELAXATION

INSTANT FOCUS

IN THE ZONE

VISUALIZATION

HYPNOSIS

DEEP SLEEP

Fig. 1. Performance enhancement skills: Performance relaxation. Created by Jack Stark.

Mental Performance

Talk/think yourself to better feelings.

Master your mind and energy so you can live your best life.

Think positively and all will be well.

If only these advertisements were that easy. How do we best get there? The Abraham-Hicks Emotional Guidance Scale illustrates the mental model of spiraling upward to perform at our best or being pulled in a downward spiral into depression and despair. The key is to take gradual steps instead of trying to jump too far too fast.

The purpose of this entire section is to provide a step-by-step approach to fully maximize our "mental game" in all three settings—work/school-play-home.

The process we use is detailed in this section of six chapters with instructions on the challenging issues, causes, and solutions to becoming an elite Top Gun performer.

Embedded in the book are six audio files designed by us to give our skills away to you. To reach your goals, practice these exercises until you can conquer your challenges and become a Top Gun performer—one who rises above others to that top 5 percent level.

The six mental skills detailed in this chapter were designed by us for individuals who want to become self-reliant and not dependent on medication or ongoing professional help.

The Research

Our research and testing of these techniques were developed over a lifetime of working with thousands of elite performers in corporations, the military, athletes at all levels, and individuals coping with the stressors of life.

The stories of success achieved by utilizing these techniques contained in these six chapters are very gratifying and far beyond our wildest expectations.

Why Audio Files?

Technology allows us to let you download each of the six audio files to your phone and practice whenever and wherever you need to. This convenience provides an *efficient, inexpensive, and powerful tool*, as so many people are not compliant with a behavioral-change program. Of the more than 50 million people in the United States who struggle with mental illness, less than half get some sort of help due to lack of time, money, and resources as well as the restrictions in their busy lives.

Our six digital audio files for Top Gun Performers will be included as aides for our readers.

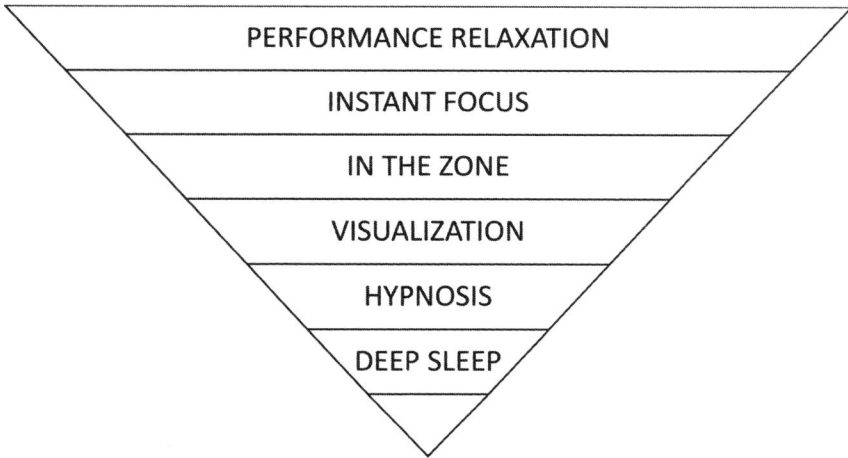

Fig. 2. Performance enhancement skills: Audio files for Top Gun performers. Created by Jack Stark.

1. PERFORMANCE RELAXATION

This nine-minute audio guide will teach you how to relax your entire body and mind by shutting down your body's reaction—to worries, distractions, expectations, and threats—and calm the body by focusing on your inner thoughts.

It is effective with individuals aged eight and up and produces, in a short time if practiced frequently, an overall calmness more powerful often than any pill.

Listen to this audio file as often as necessary, multiple times during the day and throughout the week if need be. When you first use this audio file you may become so relaxed you will fall asleep.

It is particularly effective for all the anxiety categories and pre-performance preparation.

This audio file serves as the basis and foundation for all other audio files to build from.

2. INSTANT FOCUS: BREATHING

This eight-minute audio guide is designed to rapidly increase calmness by slowing your breathing and allowing you to shut off your body's alarm system—the "fight, flight, freeze" response.

It is effective with individuals aged twelve and older (cognitive stage of understanding abstract concepts in children) and is the most powerful audio guide to address multiple performance issues.

It is designed to be a "technique" audio file whereby, after listening to the eight-minute audio guide and learning the breathing techniques, individuals often require over a hundred hours of practice to really perfect.

It is particularly effective with panic attacks and before and during competition or performance situations. It shuts down hyperventilation, which often leads to partial or full-blown panic attacks. Its use is detailed in chapter 6.

3. SELF-TALKS +/- IN THE ZONE

This ten-minute audio guide helps you shut down your negative self-talks, worries, and obsessive ruminating and replace them with positive self-talks. Using this guide improves your concentration, memory of tasks, confidence, and performance across all settings.

It builds confidence and self-esteem in individuals aged twelve and older and frees individuals from the negative downward loop that can pull them down to anxiety, then depression, and finally an inability to focus on their performance.

It is particularly effective with obsessive and compulsive thinking and the constant worrying that blocks our ability to perform. Its use is detailed in chapter 7.

4. VISUALIZATION

The ten-minute audio guide is designed to improve your mental imagery and increase your focus and concentration skills. It teaches you to shut off distractions by using all your senses, to mentally put yourself in situations where you can prepare yourself to perform.

This process creates muscle-memory activation by preparing your mind to best respond to the visual cues you are rehearsing.

It can give one an edge to perform more quickly and more accurately the behavior we see in our minds.

It works best with individuals aged twelve and older. Learning how best to perform under various situations and to react accordingly can help conquer fears and phobia by desensitizing our responses to these challenges. The technique is more deeply detailed in chapter 8.

5. HYPNOSIS—PEAK PERFORMANCE

This fourteen-minute audio file involves a deeper, more total relaxation of the body and mind. Some people use terms like meditation, mindfulness, or even deep prayer to describe this deepening process of shutting off all outside abstractions, relaxing your muscles, and breathing deeply. You are guided to visualize your best performance in the past and how best to prepare to perform against the competition in the present.

It is not a deep trance but one where you are in control of embedding positive affirmations into your subconscious to prepare you for your best performance, which you have mentally rehearsed.

It works best with individuals ages twelve and older and is especially effective for those who are irritable, restless, and depressed.

Those with trauma, post-traumatic stress disorders and neglect or abuse find that this audio file builds on and incorporates all the other audio files to be most effective.

This hypnosis audio file is a powerful way to relax and prepare for a major competitive event that will require your very best effort to reach your desired goals. Its use is more deeply detailed in chapter 9.

6. DEEP SLEEP

You can't run a car without energy of some kind.

Your body cannot perform at its best level of efficiency without the energy derived from sleep.

This nine-minute audio file promotes deep sleep by quickly shutting down your mind and body to promote healthy and natural sleeping habits of eight or more hours of solid sleep a night.

It is particularly important to get solid sleep during the week and especially the forty-eight and twenty-four hours before a competitive event requiring your maximum effort.

Sleep deprivation and insomnia are a worldwide ailment requiring a comprehensive approach without the use of sleeping pills or over-the-counter remedies that can have a negative impact on our performance—both mentally and physically.

The deep sleep technique can be used effectively with children as young as five years old. The little kids think it's cool that they get to listen to an audio file that helps them to become quiet and prepare their minds for a deeper sleep with this structured process.

A more in-depth coverage of deep sleep is covered in chapter 10.

Application of Mental Skills

The power of these six audio files that build on each other should help the talented Top Gun performers in 90 percent of the mental-physical challenges in work, athletics, and home life unless the condition is severe enough physically or mentally that it will require more intensive interventions. But even in this category, the intensity, duration, and frequency may be reduced by using these mental skills techniques.

Figure 3 contains a sample weekly chart of preparation for an event, a competition, or daily coping to maximize one's performance.

SUNDAY	MONDAY	TUESDAY	WEDNESDAY	THURSDAY	FRIDAY	SATURDAY
Time-out day. A day to get away from performing and get organized for the upcoming week. Clear your mind!	Relaxation day. Use audio file #1 "Performance Relaxation" to stay calm. During the day use in the a.m. or when there is a great deal of stress.	Relaxation and Visualization day. Listen to "Performance Relaxation" audio file #1 in the a.m. Listen to "Visualization" audio file #4 in p.m. for your performance on Saturday. Look at video or review your schedule also.	Audio file #2 on "Instant Focus" to keep heart rate down during the week to prevent exhausting yourself for weekend performance.	Relaxation in a.m. Audio file #1 and audio file #3 "Self-Talks" to reduce worries about performance on Saturday.	"Performance Relaxation" audio file #1 in a.m., audio file #3 "In the Zone" if worrisome thoughts are occurring, audio file #4 "Visualization" to visualize your best performance, and audio file #6 "Deep Sleep" to sleep the night before event.	*Event *Competition *Personal time. See one-day chart for pre-competition – the most important time in the week.

Fig. 3. Sunday–Saturday preparation. Created by Jack Stark.

CASE STUDY 1: WORK

Over the years, we have worked with national leaders and CEOs who are often called upon to make a major presentation on TV, on video, or with a live audience.

These presentations can be critical to the company and even how one is perceived to be competent.

The best example is our experience in working with local, state, congressional, and presidential candidates for a debate or major address. One slipup can be catastrophic.

The last few hours before a performance are most critical. Figure 4 shows the steps in the process I, Jack Stark, recommended for this type of event.

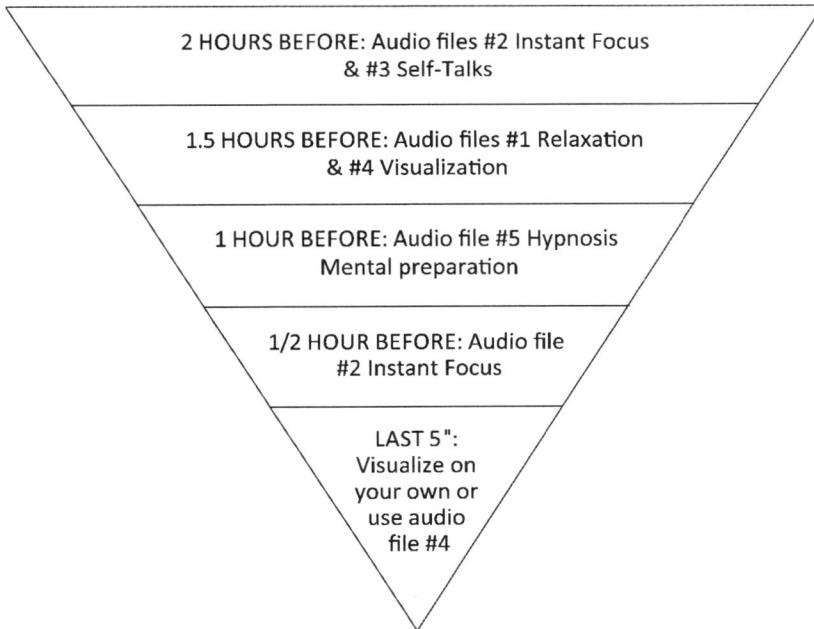

*Relaxation and Breathing Techniques may not require actually
listening to the audio files but practicing the techniques
of the audio file from your training.

Fig. 4. Two-hour preparation process for competition. Created by Jack Stark.

CASE STUDY 2: SPORTS

I was fortunate to work with a number of collegiate hockey teams and NHL players, particularly goalies, who have one of the toughest mental jobs in any sport. One goalie in particular, who was enjoyable to work with, had a long NHL career and helped me develop this technique. One small mistake can cost the team a loss. In these case studies I use the four-step mnemonic T.O.R.O.

> Tune-in (2 hours before)
> Organization zone (1½ hours before)
> Relaxation zone (1 hour before)
> Orientation zone (½ hour before)

To help this goalie to prepare each hour before a game, we developed this sample model that I have applied in my twenty-two national championship teams and thousands of athletes in multiple sports at the college and professional levels.

CASE STUDY 3: NFL RUNNING BACK

I was privileged to work with an all-American college running back who went on to become the leading running back for the Green Bay Packers.

CASE STUDY 4: NASCAR DRIVERS HENDRICK MOTORSPORTS

During my sixteen years in NASCAR, I was able to be a part of the top automotive racing teams in the world. The Hendrick Motorsports team was voted the seventh-best sports franchise of all time.

NASCAR is a unique sport that has multiple teams but only forty drivers. With so few athletes I was able to forge some amazing and close relationships with the top drivers and champions as they won the NASCAR Cup Series Drivers' Championship eight times.

NASCAR is a fascinating sport requiring mental and physical strength and a great deal of courage.

Injuries and even death were always a silent worry with drivers who go two hundred or more miles per hour into a sharp corner only inches apart. Split-second timing to know when to avoid a major wreck as well as bold passing

Tune-in zone * Organization zone * Relaxation zone * Orientation zone

4 HOURS: TUNE-IN ZONE ARRIVE AT STADIUM	• Tune-out distractions • Tune-in - FOCUS • Sweats - gear laid out - pads
2 HOURS: ORGANIZATION ZONE	• Run, warm-up • Stretching • Dress - upper gear
1 HOUR: RELAXATION ZONE	• Calm, self-hypnosis, listen #5 audio file • Breathing &visualization • Review game strategy
1/2 HOUR: ORIENTATION ZONE	• Team meeting • Coaches speak • Last-minute instructions
LAST 5 MINUTES	• Relax muscles • Deep breathing • Visualize assignments
GAME TIME!	

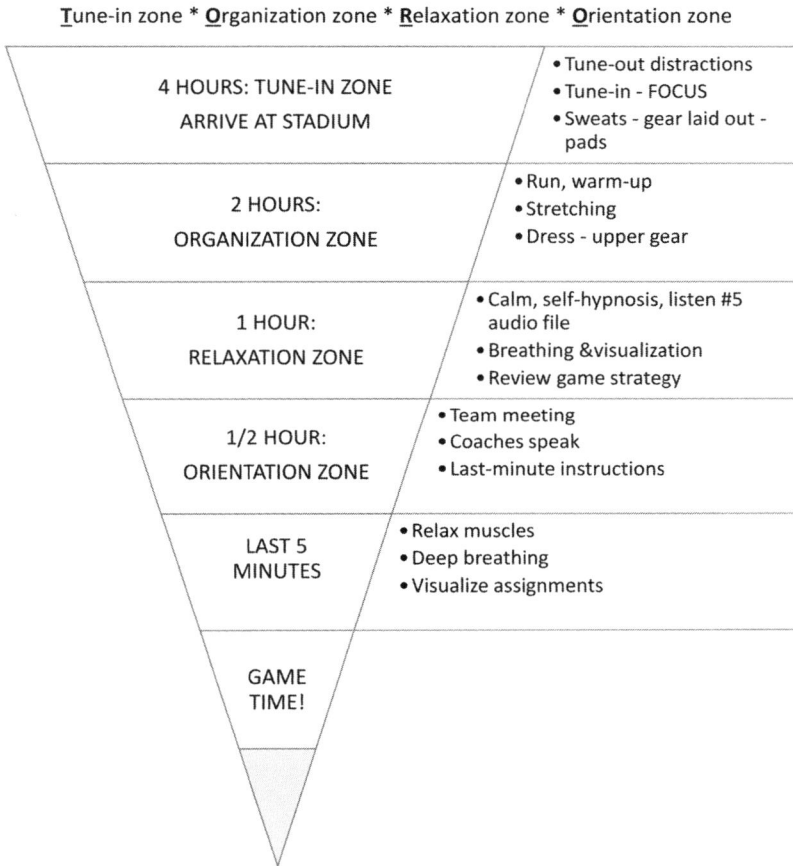

Fig. 5. Four-step mnemonic: T.O.R.O. Created by Jack Stark.

moves requires nerves of steel. This process was first introduced decades ago in a sports article.

The headline in NASCAR *Illustrated* (October 2012) was "Auto Focus: How NASCAR Stars Drive Out Distraction When It's Go Time." The weekly and race-day models are presented in figures 6 and 7 to provide another example for athletes to follow.

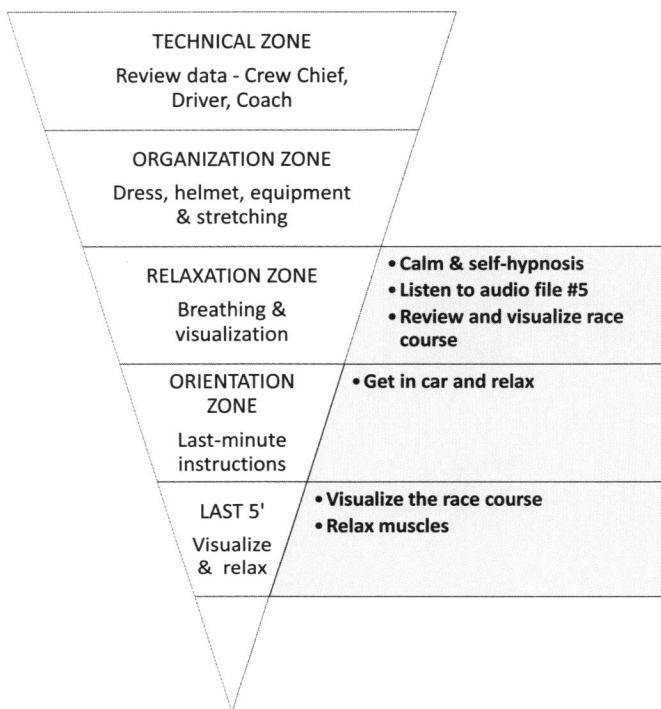

Fig. 6. NASCAR preparation. Created by Jack Stark.

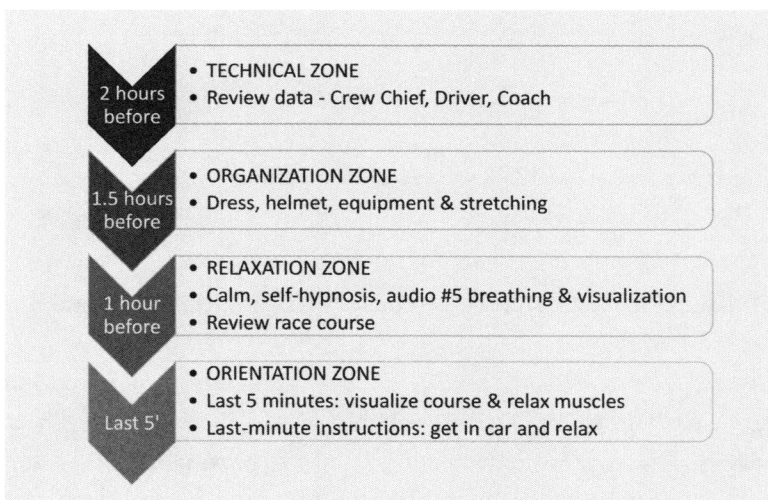

Fig. 7. NASCAR preparation: Two-hour countdown. Created by Jack Stark.

CASE STUDY 5: DE-ESCALATING CONFLICT IN OUR DAILY LIVES

In my clinical practice I often was asked to help individuals with major anger management issues to deal with conflict or to eliminate those behaviors.

My most vivid memory is of a successful de-escalation process with a six-foot-four-inch, 260-pound, former top-five world champion weightlifter in his weight class at that time. He had blown out his back in a construction job and was dealing with a lot of pain. In a multispecialty medical clinic, I was the director of medical psychology. We treated patients who suffered with pain utilizing biofeedback training.

Five minutes into our first session he stated, "If you lie to me and take the workman-comp's side, I will blow you away." Shocked, I could have dismissed him, threatened him back, or just ignored the threat. I chose instead to deal directly with him by nonchalantly saying, "Oh yeah? And how would you do that?" He responded, "With my .44 caliber magnum revolver."

"Yeah. Right. And I suppose you even have one?" thinking he was bluffing. "Would you like to see it, Doc?" "Yes, I would."

So, he took me to the parking lot, opened his trunk, and I almost fainted— the "Dirty Harry" gun was massive and took both my hands to even lift it.

My response was, "Are those hollow-point bullets here in the handgun case?" "Yes, they are, Doc." "Okay. Let's go back inside my office."

He was not bluffing.

I treated him for a few months, and we became good friends. This massive tough guy was checking me out and in one session broke down and cried over the way the pain had impacted his marriage and life. It was a good outcome with the correct initial response on my part.

The de-escalation process I employed involved staying calm, breathing deeply, and looking behind his behavior. If I had acted hostile, become angry, or refused to treat him, the outcome could have been poor for both of us.

The response I taught this champion was the same conflict de-escalation training I used with training SWAT team members and first responders in a project with Ultimate Fighting Championship, or UFC, fighters.

I served as the sports psychologist to dozens of nationally known and ranked mixed martial arts fighters. I was approached by law enforcement officers to help teach a training program in de-escalating conflict.

National and local news outlets covered high-profile cases of citizens involved in "stand your ground" cases against police interventions that resulted in death or injury of civilians. Some cases were viewed as an overreaction and resulted in lawsuits and legislation, prompting the need for this training.

CASE STUDY 6: SWAT TEAM DE-ESCALATION

De-escalating Conflict: The Three Phases

Phase 1: Precrisis

You get a call to respond to an incident and your precrisis period is the amount of time it takes to get there, or a known time you are to serve a dangerous search warrant or conduct a raid. During that period, which could be five minutes or even fifty hours before you have to respond to a call or crisis, you have to mentally prepare yourself to respond. The mental preparation period is critical to outcomes, as one can overrespond in most cases or underrespond and not be prepared for unanticipated situations.

As soon as security personnel are notified of the situation, they need to do two things: (1) get as much information *as possible* by asking questions of the referral source, and (2) review with their colleagues or within their minds how they are going to respond to a host of possible situations. Examples of conflict situations include domestic violence, disturbance calls, traffic stops, maintaining the peace, theft calls, and custody transfers.

Since law enforcement officers have a difficult time predicting all the possibilities for a proper response, their bodies go into the "fight or flight" response mode. This automatic bodily response causes the brain to send a signal to the adrenal glands, which squirt out adrenaline or cortisol, and within one-tenth of a second you can have 1,200 chemical changes. You are wired!

Your heart rate can double or triple; you may start to hyperventilate; your thinking becomes erratic; and impulsive behavior may result in an effort to assure one's safety. Know your body. Staying calm in the midst of chaos is essential for the outcome you want.

This response can be both good and bad: good that you have instant energy to react to often challenging physical situations but bad in that one may overreact, not to mention the toll this takes on one's body. Staying calm in the midst of chaos is essential for the outcome you want.

And so it is with all security personnel during practice training, as it is hard to simulate the real dangerous situations.

The key here is to *know your body*.

The Greeks, particularly Socrates, told us 2,300 years ago to *know thyself*, a phrase well worth remembering.

This phase 1, or precrisis, stage is critical to positive de-escalation outcomes. First, you get all the facts.

Second, you visualize how you are going to respond depending on a number of factors that include your training and the protocols you follow. But equally important, you need to know yourself, your mood, whether you are having issues personally or professionally that impact your behavior and may cause you to over- or underreact to a situation. It could be something at home, conflict with a supervisor, or anger over your last call.

Know your body and mind and how to de-escalate yourself before you arrive on scene in a crisis situation.

Know also that in today's environment your initial behavior is being recorded and scrutinized like never before.

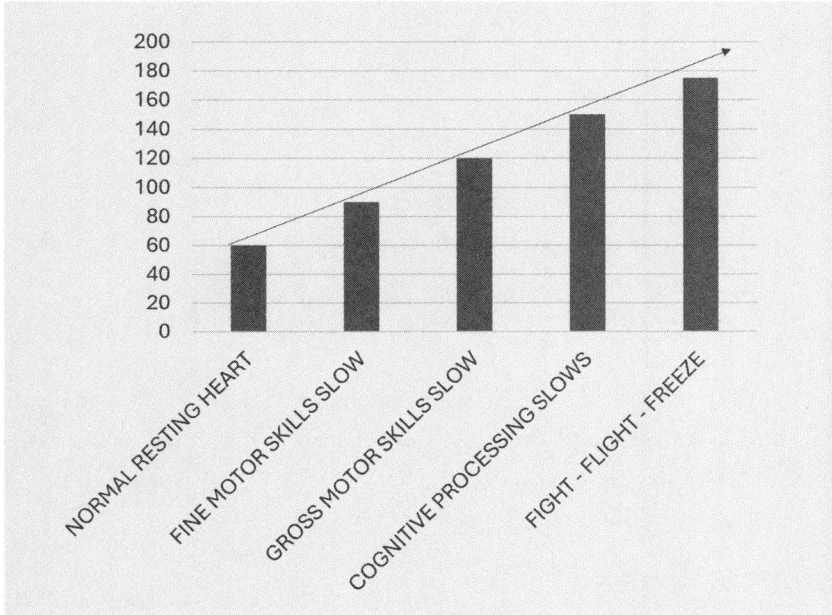

Fig. 8. Increase in heartbeats per minute (reaction slows). Created by Jack Stark.

Phase 1

Use performance relaxation (1)
Use instant focus (2)
Use self-talks (3)
Use visualization (4)

Relax during the preparation phase, which is critical to prevent overreaction and stay calm by breathing and using self-talks along with visualizing how you can best respond calmly.

Phase 2

Use instant focus to breathe and stay calm and visualize all possible scenarios during this engagement phase. Others around will react to your calm approach.

Phase 3

Use instant focus–breathing to shut off adrenaline and the sleep audio file in the nights after to let go of disturbing images and avoid PTSD aftereffects. Often your heart rate can surge after the initial adrenaline rush and intense focus of the situation is over. Coming down from this high requires such an effort in order to move on.

Top Gun Performers' Biggest Challenge: Mental Illness

Violence in the world, from wars to terrorism to shootings to crime in our communities, work, schools, and homes, dominates our headlines each day.

"Why?" you ask.

If you peel back the layers of the causes, we find that mental illness plays a dominant role.

Mental illness refers to a wide range of mental health conditions and disorders that affect our mood, thinking, and behavior in such a way as to impair normal psychological functioning.

There are six major categories of mental illness:

1. anxiety disorder,
2. mood disorder—depression,
3. schizophrenia and psychotic disorders,

4. personality disorders,
5. cognitive disorder—dementia, and
6. addictive disorder.

The exact cause of each disorder of mental illness is still not entirely known. It has become clear through research that many of these conditions are caused by a combination of genetic, biological, psychological, and environmental factors.

The World Health Organization indicates that psychological disorders far surpass many other health conditions in the world—cancer, heart disease, injuries—and, with growth over the next twenty years, will be the number-one health problem in the world.

Recent data indicates one in four individuals—25 percent in the U.S. and 36 percent in Europe—have a mental illness (NIMH). During the early 2020s, these figures spiked to 42 percent for individuals in the 18–30 age range (CDC data).

These are staggering figures, and even more of a concern is that after spending in excess of $100 billion a year on treatment, the loss from productivity is even more shocking: 35–45 percent of absenteeism from work is due to mental health problems.

EXTENT

One-third to two-thirds of serious cases of mental illness receive no treatment. Figure 9 identifies the types and percentages of mental illness expected in one's lifetime.

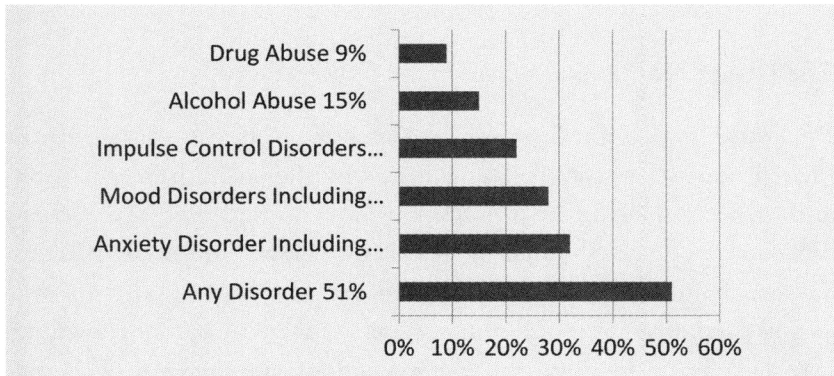

Fig. 9. Percentage of people who will have a mental illness by age seventy-five, by type of disorder. Created by Jack Stark.

The most-depressed country is Afghanistan, and the least depressed is Japan, which, to be fair, has a much more restrictive definition of mental illness than other countries do.

Top Gun performers may be reluctant to seek help, but the stigma is rapidly diminishing. The main problem is who can you see to get help? There is a shortage of psychiatrists, and they mainly treat only severe cases with medication.

My experience (having trained psychiatrists for a decade in the state's top department of psychiatry and psychiatric facility at the medical center) tells me that we desperately need more medically trained students to enter this field. Rural areas are particularly short of psychiatrists and mental health professionals.

Few if any psychiatrists are available to do psychotherapy or use the techniques described in these chapters to "give their skill away" to their clients, because insurance companies changed the reimbursement process decades ago. Further, the closure of 75 percent of psychiatric facilities in the past two decades has resulted in a shortage of beds for inpatient treatment. The transitioning of six hundred thousand individuals from state hospitals to local prisons over the past forty years has contributed to the reduction of psychotherapy by psychiatrists.

Half the PhD psychologists have also left the treatment field to enter into other areas that are better paying and less stressful. However, we have some new hope in the growth of nurse practitioners and physician assistants specializing in psychiatry.

The Use of Mental Skills Training in Psychotherapy

Psychotherapy or counseling with Top Gun performers who want to increase their mental performance skills or who have psychological challenges such as anxiety, depression, insomnia, obsessive worries, or panic attacks specifically can follow the process shown in figure 10 to increase performance and decrease emotional distress.

This psychotherapy model demonstrates the therapy process followed for over thirty years with more than ten thousand patients—most of whom were highly successful performers referred to me for "stress" reasons. The typical process for treating individuals is in phase 1, when there is hope that one's

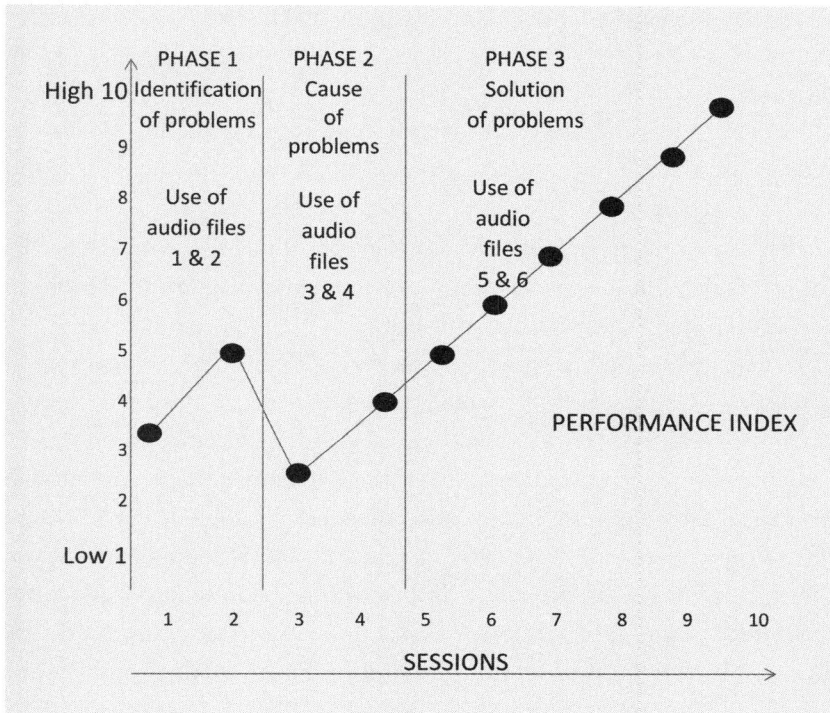

Fig. 10. Psychotherapy model. Created by Jack Stark.

problems can be solved and improvement appears by the second session. But when the causes of one's problems are analyzed, there is a brief drop in progress as issues seem daunting. This drop is necessary to reach success in phase 3, which "slingshots" one's progress as the focus shifts to finding solutions when one's skills are given away to those in need.

The referring physicians recognized that these CEOs, physicians, lawyers, and financial and business leaders needed something in addition to or beside medication. To change a person's behavior, the approach for centuries has been medication or therapy.

The results of this treatment were gratifying in that I had one of the best practices in the United States. I then used the same process to work with elite athletes at the college and professional levels who just wanted to increase their mental skills for their performance in sports and their personal lives.

This treatment process averaged ten sessions—a remarkably rapid process compared to treatment approaches by other professionals in the field that often averaged months and years.

The key to this approach was to teach these Top Gun performers how to get better via homework assignments and the use of the mental skills found in my audio files.

In phase 1 it was often found that Top Gun performers were encouraged by the first two sessions as they finally felt someone could diagnose their problem and start them on the path to getting better.

I would explain, after session 1, who they are, what they got, how they got it, and how we would solve it. I assigned audio files 1 and 2 to help them reduce the agitation and anxiety by relaxation and breathing techniques.

In phase 2 we identified the causes of their problems past and present that kept them locked into destructive patterns. Their performance level would often drop as they were reminded of all their problems and how much pain they had endured. This drop in performance resulted in some necessary but temporary feelings of doubt, which helped then in phase 3, when we were able to slingshot Top Gun performers to the solutions of their problems by helping them sleep (a major issue for almost all Top Gun performers and a major contributor to depression and anxiety) and by using hypnosis for certain performance situations.

In addition, practicing audio files 3 and 4 will teach you how to stop worrying and visualize a better path.

The result of my three-phase treatment was a thirty-year practice of fifty hours of therapy per week with no openings and being booked a month ahead. Most people got better without medication. To be clear, the research suggests that 20 percent of the population with the most challenging needs require medication, and many for years. Another 30 percent may require medication use for a brief period (less than a year), and 50 percent can benefit from other treatments and techniques without medication.

Mental Health Challenges to Top Gun Performers

Mental health experts report that half of all lifetime mental illnesses begin by age fourteen and three-quarters by age twenty-four. Suicide is the second leading cause of death for those fifteen to nineteen.

A key study by the Substance Abuse and Mental Health Services Administration on adolescents indicated the following:

50 percent of adolescents have a mental disorder, with 22 percent having severe impairment.

32 percent had an anxiety disorder, the rate being higher for females than for males.

17 percent of students underwent treatment for anxiety in college (American College Health Association).

13 percent had had at least one major depressive disorder.

40 percent of college students in general and student-athletes in particular exhibited a mental disorder.

The difference in outcomes is that sports provides a system of structure, rules, consistency, and reinforcement for appropriate behavior along with *the power of exercise*—a huge impact on preventing or decreasing depression and anxiety for everyone (analysis of thirty studies, University of Ireland, *Journal of the American Medical Association*).

Use of Medication: Be Cautious

Michael Phelps, the most decorated Olympic swimmer ever, tells his story of locking himself in his bedroom for four days after being arrested for DUI. He was depressed and thought of suicide.

Today many college and professional athletes are speaking out on their struggles with mental illness.

Incredibly talented Top Gun performers may be ever more susceptible to stress and pressure due to the high expectations and demands they face daily.

The shortage of professionals to treat mental illness and the staggering needs as described above have resulted in a significant increase in the use of medication.

Most medications today are prescribed by primary-care, family-practice, or internal-medicine physicians.

I saw these physicians, having worked in the hallways with them for thirty years, often having to see forty to fifty patients a day, averaging ten to fifteen minutes per person. It varies, but national surveys indicate an average of fifteen minutes per visit. No one wants this situation, but the shortage of mental health professionals, coupled with the explosive growth in mental health cases, has resulted in these challenges.

Therapy takes more time and can cost more—but is just as effective as medication in many cases. Meta research over the past twenty years is clear: psychotherapy and the use of the mental-skill training in these chapters (cognitive behavioral therapy techniques) is as effective as medication, or even more so, in the majority of cases.

Diagnosis is also a major issue—40 percent of all cases are misdiagnosed. Medication works in only 60 percent of cases, according to research.

Antidepressants can take up to three to four weeks to work, and because it's often difficult to determine which one of the meds works best, patients undergo trials of numerous antidepressants.

The top-ten most-prescribed mental health medications currently are

1. Zoloft (depression),
2. Xanax (anxiety—highly addictive and lethal when mixed with other pain medications),
3. Lexapro (depression),
4. Celexa (depression),
5. Wellbutrin (depression),
6. Desyrel (anxiety, depression, and insomnia),
7. Prozac (depression),
8. Adderall (attention deficit disorder [ADD]),
9. Ativan (anxiety), and
10. Cymbalta (depression).

Every medicine has risks, even aspirin. But drugs can be a powerful treatment choice, especially for non-mental-health issues. The side effects of antidepressants range from a low percentage to a much higher percentage depending on the individual.

Mental Toughness

No book on mental performance would be complete without a comment on mental toughness. Everyone wants it, or they want others to have it.

The difficulty is that the definition differs depending on its application to various situations.

The best definition I found was offered by a national championship soccer coach, Elmer Bolowich, who said, "Mental toughness is the ability to perform at the upper range of your capabilities regardless of competitive circumstances."

The words "grit" and "resilience" are perhaps most descriptive. An example of mental toughness can be found in the life of Abraham Lincoln, the greatest president in the history of the United States and who had a profound impact on American history (Goodwin 2018). Lincoln overcame so many challenges yet persevered to achieve greatness.

Difficult childhood
Political defeats—six
Deaths of two sons
Nervous breakdown at age twenty-seven
Deep depression and loneliness
Mediocre marriage
President at age fifty-one
Assassinated at age fifty-six

One can also visualize Michael Jordan, the greatest NBA player, scoring forty-five points on a night he took intravenous fluids for the flu.

My best definition is of a single mother with three kids. One of the kids was visually and auditorily impaired.

She got up each morning early, drove her son one hour to the state school for deaf and blind students, drove home, and got her other two kids to school. Then she went to work and repeated the process after work.

One thing is for sure—mental toughness is evolving. The days of Vince Lombardi–style coaching, or leading by yelling or even swearing and challenging individuals, are over.

I often used to ask athletes, "How do you want to be coached?" Twenty years ago, most answered, "I can handle any style." Today very few respond to negative motivation. Research shows the best motivation for mental toughness comes not from anger, fear, or revenge but from a close bond and caring for others.

A 2017 study of inner-city teenagers in a rough Chicago neighborhood showed that those with the ability to suppress intrusive and unpleasant thoughts and demonstrate resilience to threatening situations had a healthier brain in the areas that govern regulation of emotion (Miller, Chen, and Parker 2017).

Individuals exposed to and trained by others in early childhood to be mentally tougher developed healthier brains. Mental toughness is a learned trait that is reinforced by one's environment and can be enhanced in an organization, a sports team, and a family. This chapter recognized the power of performance relaxation and serves as the basis for the building of the additional five mental performance skills.

6

Instant Focus

Controlling the breath is a prerequisite to controlling the mind and the body.
—HIMALAYAN INSTITUTE

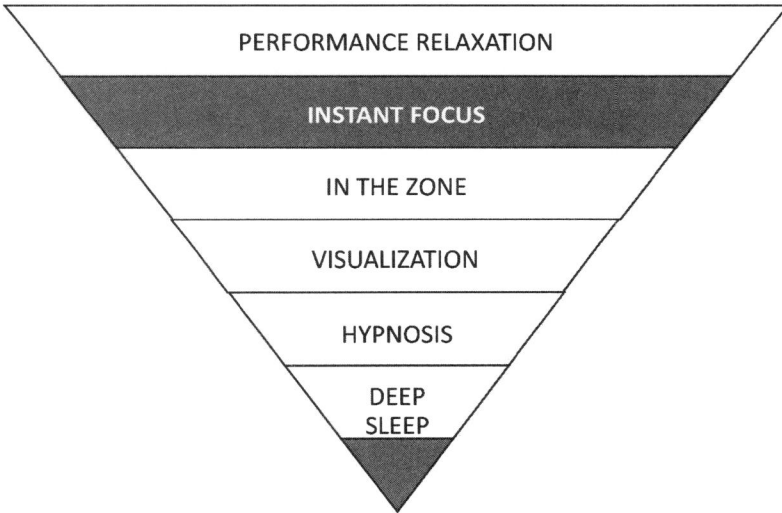

Fig. 11. Performance enhancement skills: Instant focus. Created by Jack Stark.

We are often asked, "What is the single most important mental skill that enhances performance?" Answer: breathing for instant focus.

The response at first by various Top Gun performers is puzzlement. It sounds so simple to breathe properly. I, Dr. Stark, explain that I can tell you how to best perform this physical-mental skill in ten minutes, but it can take one hundred hours of practice to perfect it.

A perfect example of the use of this mental skill occurred in San Antonio during the second round of the NCAA basketball tournament in March 2014.

I was attending the tournament as part of the Creighton University basketball team and was interviewed for my work with national player of the year Doug McDermott. Interviewers Steve Kerr (now head coach of the Golden State Warriors) and Marv Albert were covering the tournament for the TNT TV network.

They were interested in knowing about my work with the three-time all-American player, especially our pregame routine of hypnosis and relaxation. Marv was joking and asked if I could fix Steve Kerr's golf game. I was impressed with Kerr, and shortly thereafter, he went on to coach the Warriors and win championships.

I explained some mental tips for putting in golf and how to avoid the "yips," that is, choking, tightening up, and struggling to perform. Then I explained how I also used this same technique of breathing to shoot free throws. Kerr was really interested in this area as a former sharpshooter for the national champion Chicago Bulls with Michael Jordan. I demonstrated the technique of breathing to help him make his free throws consistently.

I got a text from him one week later. He said, "Man, where were you in my career, as this really helped my percentage of free throws? I could have used you back then."

Controlling the breath and calming the nerves are prerequisite to controlling the mind—and control of the mind is a prerequisite to elite performance.

Why Focus on Breathing?

I had an occasion to hear the great poet, author, and humanitarian Maya Angelou give a presentation. To listen to the story of her life's journey and the way she looked at the world illustrates how she became a Top Gun performer.

Angelou once said, "Life is not measured by how many breaths we take, but by the moments that take our breath away." Eloquence that grabs a person's soul!

It is important to know that, on average, a person at rest takes about sixteen breaths per minute. This means we breathe about 960 breaths an hour, 23,040 breaths a day, and 8,409,600 breaths a year.

Obviously if we engage in vigorous exercise that number will dramatically increase. You take up to twenty breaths a minute while lounging on the couch and four times as many during intense treadmilling.

If we live to age eighty, we will have taken a whopping 672,768,000 breaths in our lifetime.

The Purpose of Breath

The primary purpose of breath is to move oxygen into your bloodstream and at the same time remove carbon dioxide from the blood and into the air. Our lungs don't have the muscles for pumping air into and out of our lungs—so our diaphragm and rib cage must do the work.

People normally use only about 70 percent of their lung capacity (Kingsley 2024). If our lungs were open flat, they would cover the size of an entire tennis court.

Very few people are aware of their breathing patterns and have almost no knowledge of how the breath impacts our health and performance. Our breathing is often erratic, as we tend to be breath-holders depending on our activity and stress levels. If our breathing is erratic or stressed, reduced access to oxygen results in stale air being trapped inside the lungs, which can lead to numerous respiratory illnesses.

I once had a fifty-six-year-old male patient with heart disease whose breathing pattern involved only his chest moving in a short, abrupt, choppy breathing pattern. His pattern made me uncomfortable, as I realized how quickly it impacted my own breathing pattern—slowly in and slowly out. I wanted to scream, "Breathe!"

Yet when we look at infants, we notice the natural process of abdominal breathing—watching the bellies move up and down with every breath.

Breath and Heart Rate

Breath has a powerful and immediate impact on our entire body and can best be measured by our heart rates. A perfect example is the story of a top college football player—one of the best kickers in the country.

I put a heart monitor on his chest, and when I woke him up at 7 a.m., his heart rate was 50 beats per minute. He was in great athletic shape. His rate was 60 at the time of the pregame chapel service, 70 at breakfast, and 80 in my car going to the stadium.

It was 90 in the locker room, 110 during warm-ups, and 120 during game time, and when he went in to kick the winning forty-three-yard field goal, his heart rate peaked at 140 beats per minute. He kicked the winning field goal in the last three seconds against Colorado to win the game. He went on to have a long career in the NFL.

Remarkably, 50 at bedrest and 140 at the most excitable moment requires an ability to slow down your heart rate for peak performance. Being able to "instantly calm" oneself is a huge edge. It cuts across all areas of work—sports and daily life.

Heart rate is the most efficient and easy way to measure one's excitability. Using a chest belt, watch, or phone app, or just checking your own pulse via the wrist or carotid artery, gives you a measure of exertion the heart requires to meet your energy demands.

The average heart rate is between 60 and 100 beats per minute. At the average of 75 beats per minute, the average person's heart beats 108,000 times a day or approximately 40 million times per year.

Breathing for relaxation can significantly reduce the frequency of heartbeats and improve health and performance. Control of one's breath is the single most important factor in producing instant relaxation for peak performance.

The Use of the Polygraph

A polygraph, popularly referred to as a lie detector, is used to measure and record several physiological indicators.

These physical indicators measure our emotional response to questions:

1. respiration—rate of breathing,
2. blood pressure,
3. pulse—heart rate, and
4. skin conductivity.

Having practiced deep-breathing exercises for thirty-five years, I was surprised in taking a polygraph test how easy it was to fool the test just by controlling my breath—respiration.

It allowed me to keep my heart rate and blood pressure all normal, but I could not control skin conductivity. This is the process of using small electrical probes to measure the opening and closing of my skin pores to secrete perspiration. It is so instantaneous that it seems to be the hardest to control.

People who engage in deep breathing exercises during meditation three to four times a day, however, have a remarkable ability to control many physiological responses of the body, including those measured with a polygraph.

The Physiology and Psychology of Breath

Breathing is the only physiological process that can be either voluntary or involuntary. Individuals can breathe consciously, making the breath do whatever they wish; or they can ignore it and the body breathes on its own.

We have learned about the power of breath from yogis, especially yogis from India. A yogi is a practitioner of yoga, which means "to join" or "to unite" the mind and body, especially those who became masters via their daily practice of *svarodaya*, the science of breath.

THE NOSE

The nose does so much more than simply let air in. Medical specialists in this area (rhinologists) or ENTs (ear, nose, and throat specialists) can list nearly thirty distinct functions that it performs.

It filters, moisturizes, directs air flow, warms air, registers the sense of smell, brings in oxygen, creates mucus, provides a route of drainage for sinuses, and has a powerful impact on the nervous system (Rama 1998).

SINUS CAVITIES

There are five sinus cavities:

1. left front sinus,
2. right front sinus,

3. left maxillary sinus,

4. right maxillary sinus, and

5. sphenoidal sinus.

To maximize performance, it is important to avoid sinus infections or blockages. Ever try to perform with a stuffy or runny nose? It is twice as difficult to breathe, and labored breathing promotes fatigue.

TURBINATES

The most prominent structures of the nasal cavity are three seashell-like bulges one can see if we look up inside the nose. These turbinates' function is to stir and circulate the air as it enters the nose. They impact the moisture content and temperature of the air.

As the air leaves the lungs, the opposite reaction occurs—cool and dry coming in and warm and moist going out. In addition, the turbinates are covered with a mucous membrane that secretes mucus to pick up dust and debris and carry it out of the nose.

Oxygen in the atmosphere moves from the nose or mouth down the trachea through the bronchial system. The oxygen is absorbed into the bloodstream flowing through the capillaries.

It came as a shock to me to discover, as I practice deep breathing, that one nostril is more open than the other and they switch back and forth depending on our emotional state. The goal, hard to attain, is to equalize the airflow in both nostrils.

If you try closing one nostril and breathe, you will discover one side is slightly more open than the other. The left side open often indicates more passiveness and a psychological state that focuses on inner relaxation, whereas the right side may indicate more emotion, being more active, aggressive, alert, and focused on the external world. The old scriptural readings of meditation indicate that it is best to eat when the right nostril is open.

Healthy Nose: Maximize Performance

I have long been an advocate of the power of rhythmic breathing. I was first introduced to these techniques some forty years ago by an extraordinary PhD

Fig. 12. The neti pot. Courtesy Jack Stark.

psychologist who practiced meditation daily and engaged in deep breathing exercises throughout the day.

I was amazed at his calming effect and noted that he always had such a positive and peaceful personality. He had studied at the Himalayan Institute with some talented physicians and yogis—particularly Swami Rama.

He introduced me to the use of the neti pot. At first, like many, I thought that using a cleansing technique was a little "gross." Then I started using the neti pot and since then have rarely missed using this technique upon waking up and before going to bed. Also, if I have been working outside and it's dusty or if I have a cold, then I use the pot more often.

I recall teaching and lecturing to an entire medical school class about stress and introduced the concept of the neti pot. The students became so enthusiastic that we handmade via pottery one neti pot for each of the 150 medical students as a token of the class experience.

The yoga manual describes a technique called jala neti (purification with water). The process involves pouring a measured amount of sea salt into lukewarm distilled or sterile water in the pot. Distilled water is purified water from which minerals and impurities have been removed. It is water that has been boiled into vapor and condensed back into liquid in a separate container. You can drink this water but won't like the taste as it is flatter and less flavorful than tap water. Most tap waters are safe to use, but it's best to be cautious to prevent infections and *always* be careful not to use well water, which may contain harmful bacteria that can infect the sinus cavities and the brain itself.

Use one-quarter teaspoon of 99 percent pure noniodized salt. Then pour it into each nostril alternately by tilting your head sideways for each side.

Be sure to let all the water drain out of your sinus by tilting your head forward and side to side, or later as you bend over, a few drops may come out of the sinus cavities they had pooled in.

This lukewarm, saline water not only dissolves and washes away any accumulated mucus and dirt, but it also, by osmosis, draws out excess water from swollen turbinate structures. And most important, it facilitates drainage of the sinuses.

In the 1980s and 1990s I was embedded in the internal medicine department of a large medical clinic as the director of behavioral medicine. The internist and ear, nose, and throat doctors referred patients to me for chronic sinusitis. They would tell the docs, "Hey, we need those neti pots that Dr. Stark started us on." "The sinus antibiotics pills don't work as well as the neti pot."

If you think about it, if one takes an antibiotic pill, it gets dissolved into the bloodstream and tries to unblock or open the tiny sinus openings—particularly the hard-to-get-to sphenoid sinus. I have only rarely had a sinus infection over the past forty years using the neti pot.

The use of the neti pot and a simple saline (saltwater) one-and-a-half-ounce nasal spray available at any drugstore for a few dollars is especially helpful during the day or while flying.

Air during the winter and in dry climates is heated and dried out. The use of humidifiers and nasal sprays, along with frequent use of the neti pot, will drastically reduce sinus infections and colds and increase performance.

A perfect example of this was during a recent vacation to the Cayman Islands. The hotel staff recommended having my grandkids, who get frequent colds, dunk themselves in the ocean: "The sea salt helps to cleanse the nose!"

Types of Breath

There are many types of breathing, and breathing exercises, for optimal health and performance. But for 99 percent of Top Gun performers, learning to do the best and most physiologically efficient breathing technique will provide you with dramatic results.

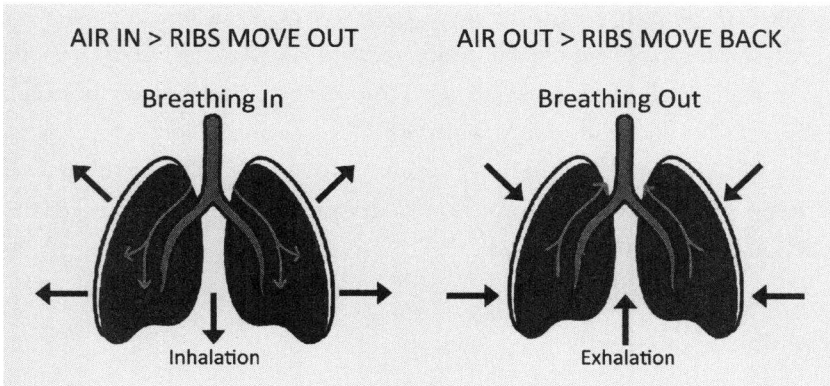

Fig. 13. Air in, air out. Created by Jack Stark.

Universally recognized by practitioners and researchers, the *diaphragmatic breathing technique* is an essential skill to control your mind and body.

The diaphragm is a large muscle that separates the chest cavity from the abdomen. It is the main muscle for breathing. Contraction of the diaphragm muscle expands the lungs during inspiration when one is breathing air in, and relaxation of the diaphragm happens when one exhales.

The key to efficient breathing is to utilize the lower lungs, as that is where the blood is enriched by air in the capillaries. It is interesting that infants and small children use their diaphragms exclusively for breathing.

Yet most adults lose the efficient diaphragmatic process by engaging in chest and shoulder breathing, which is choppy and less efficient. Chest and shoulder breathing requires more work to accomplish the same blood/gas mixing than the slow, deep diaphragmatic breathing. More work, more oxygen, more frequent breaths equals less efficiency and puts more stress on the cardiovascular system.

The best way to learn this incredible technique is to lie down and place something light on your belly. As you breathe in visualize air coming into your belly and filling your abdomen.

Obviously, the air actually fills the lower portion of your lungs by contracting your diaphragm on inhalation and relaxing your diaphragm on exhalation. By slowing your breathing and using the diaphragm you will instantly begin to feel the calming effects on the body.

The belly should raise and lower itself in a slow rhythmic process. When we breathe more rapidly or hold our breath, we send signals to the rest of our body that not all is well, and we need to be on the alert versus relaxed and peaceful.

Controlling the breath and calming the nerves are a prerequisite to controlling the mind. And control of the mind is a prerequisite to Top Gun performance.

Remember, Top Gun performers—all acts are first mental and precede the physical if even by microseconds.

The Power of Breath

Of all the techniques, medicine, tools, training, and strategies to help Top Gun performers, the most powerful of all is *breathing*. That sounds crazy and way too simplistic. But it's not just breathing; it's the proper and most efficient breathing. It is not as easy as it sounds. I can explain the entire process in ten minutes, but it can take one hundred or more hours to learn and perfect.

Breathing efficiently does not get a lot of attention, perhaps because it is free, safe, simple, and taken for granted, or because people have not been trained in its effectiveness and use. Think of how many times during the day we have to deal with negative thoughts, phone calls, tweets, emails, conversations, or disturbing news that sends signals to our body to be alert, to react. The numbers of negative signals unfortunately today far exceed our positive signals.

I have never been pulled over for driving under the speed limit and offered a free Big Mac hamburger, but if I exceed the speed limit the chances are I will be fined. We try to avoid the negatives of life. But what can we do if they happen? Answer: control our nervous system.

The Nervous System

The nervous system coordinates all the functions of our body and is subdivided into the central and the autonomic nervous systems.

The *central nervous* system consists of the brain, twelve pairs of cranial nerves, the spinal cord, and thirty-one pairs of spinal nerves that spread throughout the body.

The *autonomic nervous* system (think automatic) is an involuntary spontaneous or unconscious system that is further divided into the sympathetic and parasympathetic systems.

These two subsystems work in seeming opposition to each other, yet the final result is a harmonious regulation.

SYMPATHETIC

The sympathetic system accelerates the heart. It is the "go" button for the fight, flight, or freeze mechanism.

PARASYMPATHETIC

The parasympathetic system slows down the heart. Activation of this "stop" button means that we are calmer, have lower blood pressure, digest food better, and produce less inflammation.

Balance between the two systems helps with relaxation and our blood glucose levels, and cholesterol levels are better regulated. Blood pressure and symptoms of cardiovascular disease, stroke, and diabetes, among other things, are all improved.

Research is now focused on the vagal nerve, which descends from the brain, impacts the heart and gut in digestion, and calms the body. Vagal tone, as it is called, has a powerful impact for improving

1. anxiety disorder,
2. post-traumatic stress disorder,
3. cognitive issues—alertness, focus, memory,
4. migraines, and
5. depression.

A landmark study published in the *American Journal of Psychiatry* followed 795 treatment-resistant depression patients for five years. Forty-three percent of those who used medication, therapy, and vagus nerve stimulation experienced remission of their depression, whereas only 26 percent of those who received only medication and therapy had remission.

Breathing Techniques and Biofeedback

In the 1970s, 1980s, and 1990s, medicine was focused on the traditional techniques of surgery, medication, or use of medical procedures with an emphasis on the physician doing something to the patient. Giving a pill takes only a few minutes, and patients were dependent on the prescription process.

I wanted to change this process via behavioral medicine techniques of helping patients, clients, and particularly athletes to avoid pills and their side effects by teaching self-control techniques via biofeedback, if possible.

Bio. Body feedback through body measurements was popular but not covered by insurance and thus never really took off in this country. However, I found it to be powerful as an adjunct to therapy.

Pain. Muscle tension feedback via temperature measurements increases blood flow to certain parts of the body.

Anxiety and panic attacks. The use of diaphragmatic breathing was powerful and by far the most effective nonmedication treatment. Meds have side effects, and anxiety medications (benzodiazepines) can be addictive.

Phobias. Deep breathing on a progressive exposure to the fear to break down the stressors was particularly effective.

Post-traumatic stress disorder. Reliving the traumatic experience by doing deep diaphragmatic breathing was very effective at diminishing the trauma, again without medication.

All of my patients via clinical practice (ten thousand), clients in corporations (one hundred companies), and high school, college, and pro athletes (eight thousand) over the past forty years have benefited from the use of the audio file on instant focus and relaxation—focused diaphragmatic breathing.

Biofeedback: The Menninger Clinic

I wish I could tell the readers of this book that I was smart enough on my own to get exposure to the Eastern medicine techniques of relaxation and the science of breathing with the experts at the Himalayan Institute, but it was only by hiring a PhD psychologist who interned at the Himalayan Institute and brought his knowledge to our biofeedback clinic at the University of Nebraska Medical Center. For ten years at the med center and twenty years in private practice, with his teachings I was able to perfect what at the time was considered "fluff" but is now mainstream in all medical schools.

It was during these earlier years that we in the department of psychiatry were also exposed to the research at the Menninger Clinic. The Menninger Clinic was established in 1925 and became the premier psychiatric clinic in the country.

I became familiar with the clinic in the 1990s as we referred a number of elite college athletes for evaluation and treatment. These were athletes who often went on to play for many years in the NFL, the NBA, and the NHL.

There was a section at the clinic doing research on biofeedback and break-throughs in alternative medicine techniques. A top-notch team of MDs and PhDs developed portable biofeedback and physiological measurement machines, which they took to India to study Eastern medicine techniques.

Their focus was on how these holy men—yogis and swamis—could exhibit incredible ability to control the body through their powerful mental techniques developed from years of yoga, meditation, and breathing exercises. The researchers challenged the traditional views of medicine in this area.

Their main focus was on the most holy Hindu male religious teacher in India, who rose to level of "swami." Focusing on the heart, they hooked up the swami to an electrocardiograph and numerous other devices. He then went into a deep trance of relaxation and breathing and indicated that he could make his heart skip a beat on command—which he did to their astonishment.

He then indicated that he would release the "dove" in his chest, and his heart rate went from fifty to two hundred beats per minute. His heart essentially quivered, and the electrocardiogram was shown to a cardiologist who asked, "This man was having a heart attack, and did he survive?" The team answered, "No heart attack. He was just fine after he brought his heart back to normal rhythm after a few minutes."

Preposterous, you say! I frequently, over many years, played the video and audio file of this experiment for our medical students to document the power of the mind controlled by diaphragmatic breathing and meditation.

A second video shown to the medical students was of an individual from the Netherlands who was a frequent practitioner of the same techniques. He too was hooked up to a heart monitor (EKG), an electroencephalograph (EEG), and additional biological measures.

He touched his left arm and declared that he had made that arm numb and "detached" it from his body to feel no pain. He then stabbed an eight-inch metal needle through his bicep. The needle, which had been used in sewing canvas and was rusty, went through his bicep and stuck out the other side. After five seconds he withdrew the needle and only a drop of blood came out; no infection or pain was registered on the equipment.

His heart rate and EEG findings were normal throughout. Again, it was an amazing feat of control—perhaps flooding his arm with his own endorphins and encephalons, the body's natural pain killer.

These experiments served to illustrate that while these were two exceptional individuals with decades of practice, we could all benefit from the lesson that we are capable of having more control over our body if we can tune into mental techniques described in this chapter.

To illustrate this process, let's focus on the application and use of this audio file and its powerful benefits.

Instant Focus: Breathing

Audio file 2 is an eight-minute audio recording designed to teach Top Gun performers the critical skill of being able to "instantly relax." If your muscles are tight, your heart is pounding, and you have butterflies in your stomach, it is difficult to perform at your very best.

This is especially true for Top Gun performers where one play, one person, one game or one comment, one minute can change your lifetime or the viability of an entire company or the viability of an entire team. You live in a world where a small 1–5 percent difference in performance is so critical—you win or lose a game or miss your financial projections and careers are impacted.

This audio file and chapter were designed to teach this critical skill of breathing to bring about instant focus and relaxation to perform a challenging task.

This breathing skill is a critical tool that is utilized in every audio file and chapter in this book. What was considered "fluff" thirty years ago is now so mainstream that every recommendation from all practitioners for dealing with stress and performance make it their top priority.

Only good can come from it. There are no bad side effects, expensive costs, or difficulty with use or availability. It's a skill that even little kids can and should use. Better health and happiness are the result once you are able to relearn this technique that was natural to us at birth but later changed for many of us into a bad habit of holding our breath or hyperventilating.

Audio file tips:

1. Focused breathing involves breathing in through your nose and breathing out through your mouth.
2. Use a four-second count of breathing in (1-2-3-4) and breathing out (1-2-3-4) in an even count.
3. Breathe in by filling your stomach, which allows the diaphragm muscle to relax and let more air come into the lower portion of your lungs, which are more blood enriched than the upper portion.
4. Visualize a bell-shaped curve of slowly breathing in and out *evenly*.
5. Use an eight-count "cleansing breath" to rid the lungs of stale air by breathing in while counting to four, filling your stomach, then going for another four-second count by moving up to fill your middle and upper chest. Slowly exhale by first releasing the chest, then down to your stomach.
6. If you are able to do an eight-count cleansing breath to *start*, followed by ten separate and rhythmic four-count breaths, then *finish* with another eight-count cleansing breath, you will feel as if you just took a tranquilizing pill.

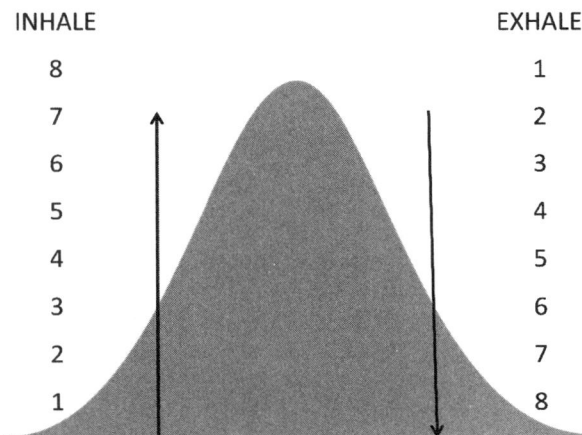

INHALE   EXHALE

INHALE	EXHALE
8	1
7	2
6	3
5	4
4	5
3	6
2	7
1	8

Fig. 14. Inhale/exhale curve. Created by Jack Stark.

It works that fast. Your fingers may even tingle! The blood that was pushed out by the stress signals rushes back into your hands, which now become warm, an indication of relaxation.

F.O.C.U.S. Technique

This powerful technique utilizes breathing and relaxation via this mnemonic five-word reminder of the demanding task you are about to perform.

F: *Forget*—let go of all distractions in your mind.
O: *Organize*—get yourself physically ready to perform.
C: *Concentrate*—visualize the task you are about to perform.
U: *Unwind*—use your four- or eight-count deep breathing to instantly relax your body.
S: *Shoot/Speak/Step*—as you perform the act, you breathe out to relax all your muscles, so you are not tight by holding your breath.

Think of the terms "yips," "choke," "panic." Top Gun performers tell me:

Doc, I squeezed the hockey stick and drove the puck over the top of a wide-open net.
I was relaxed until I stepped up to putt for the championship and tightened up—I can't control my yips.
I froze when I stepped in front of the microphone to speak.
I felt the instant rush of panic with the game on the line to shoot a simple free throw and shot an air ball.

I recommend becoming proficient in this breathing technique by practicing throughout the day many times. It will significantly improve both your health and performance. It only takes a few minutes but produces amazing results.

Application of Instant Focus

Below are practical and amazingly effective uses of this skill in all three areas, along with specific stories of successful application.

SCHOOL

Depression rates have spiked by 33 percent in the past five years. Headline news of national survey data reveals that loneliness and lack of meaningful relationships in our lives are at an all-time high. Stress levels are through the roof, and technology and social media make life even more complex and difficult to navigate. Most of all, we hear from all our clients that the pace and speed of constant change creates a consuming state of constant worry (Zhao et al. 2023).

We often point out to Top Gun performers that there are only two types of people in the world—those who have made it and worry that they can lose it and those who have not made it and afraid that they will never make it. We are all worried! Our brains are hardwired to be most peaceful when we can predict things. Our parents worked at one job their entire life, our grandchildren will work at dozens of jobs in multiple settings and even countries, requiring lifelong learning and adaptability. Learning to control these stressors with such powerful tools combined in this book, especially the ability to instantly focus via a simple, efficient breathing technique can help all of us to navigate these challenges.

SPORTS

One of the most effective uses of instant focus has been in the game of golf. Everyone has heard of the concept of "the yips." This is a term coined for people who choke, tighten up, and struggle to perform, particularly in putting. I attended the 2016 Olympics in Rio de Janeiro and met a golfer representing his country. A talented athlete as a youth, he attended college on a scholarship and was able to make the PGA tour—barely at first. Approximately 125 players are on the elite PGA tour. He was most interested in improving his putting as a few-stroke improvement could make all the difference in his game, especially to make the "cut" for the final two days of the tournaments throughout the year. After six months of practice with me at first and later just using the audio file exercises, he significantly improved his putting skills. Remarkably he was listed in the top ten of the entire tour for putting, something Tiger Woods would love to accomplish. This process is easy to explain but hard to learn and can take a hundred hours to perfect. Why? Because we develop subtle bad habits that interfere with performance. Our breathing patterns are almost all nondiaphragmatic, or nonabdominal, and are short, choppy, and irregular. Such patterns result in a tightening of our bodies, particularly the forearms. As we putt, we can relax during our warmup-practice putts, but the minute we stand over the golf ball, we tighten our muscles and *hold our breath*, thus our putt is no longer smooth, fluid, and relaxed. The result is a "herky-jerky" motion particularly on key tension-filled moments when we have to perform. Golfers, pay attention to the slight tightness of your forearms and abdominal muscles during the putt. Notice how this slight tightening throws the alignment off your stroke. The key is to take a deep breath to relax all your muscles on exhaling. Then breathe in again slowly, and as you exhale slowly using the one-to-four count, perform your entire putt. When you breathe out (exhale), your abdominal muscles, arms legs, and so forth also relax. This key five-second process of slow inhalation and kick, shoot, putt, or throw on exhalation is absolutely critical to your success in all sports.

With baseball and softball players, I like to get inside the batting cage and observe their behavior. Remember, your personality is where I start, whereas 99 percent of coaches focus on form and body mechanics, spending lots of money and time on video analysis while ignoring how you "think." The mental always precedes the physical. The personality type is usually one of being a perfectionist, not wanting to fail, trying to please everyone, and often playing to avoid the pain of losing versus embracing the joy of winning. I worked with a college baseball player and an all-state high-school softball player. After observing the swing of the bat, I could clearly see they were trying too hard— squeezing the bat so hard you could see their white knuckles. I asked them to take normal swings, and the result was a lot of grounders, fouls, and pop-ups. Next I instructed them to take a deep breath, in and out, to relax. Then breathe in and slowly out to relax the body while they stood at the plate. Then breathe in, then out slowly, and on the exhale just relax and meet the ball. Just be fluid. The result was tears of joy and a significant increase in their batting percentages and a scholarship for the softball player.

I had a top collegiate kicker at a Power 5 school who was in a slump. He often held his breath, tightened up, and "punched the ball," resulting in missed low-trajectory kicks. Antianxiety medication helped some, but there were side effects, so he stopped taking it. I helped him *instantly relax* via breathing, whereby he would take a deep breath in and relax his entire body and then exhale all the tightness. Then he would breathe in as he began his step and breathe out as he swung his leg to connect with the ball. He went on to be player of the year in the Canadian Football League a few years later.

In soccer, think about those few five-second moments when you have to perform. A star high-school athlete, and now a physician, used these techniques during a scissors kick in the last few minutes of his final high school game to win the state championship, a skill that requires perfect timing and relaxation. Corner kicks, penalty kicks, shoot-outs all require that *instant relaxation* for the perfect shot. Interestingly, I treated a Hungarian soccer player who explained to me that during his team's 1956 Olympic game, the coach taught them how to use *diaphragmatic breathing* while running, a difficult task, as we all become chest (clavicular) breathers during exertion, particularly running. The Europeans have always emphasized the mental game, as they lack the facilities and the nutritional, strength, and conditioning staff that richer countries use.

My first Ultimate Fighting Championship (UFC) fighter was an ex-all-American collegiate wrestler and former marine. Tough. It was his first fight in the UFC series versus other sanctioned mixed martial arts programs. He was mismatched against a top-five world-ranked jujitsu fighter. I conducted my prefight relaxation training and the use of instant focus audio files in preparation for the fight. I was sitting with a group of UFC fighters I also had trained. In the first round he knocked the jujitsu fighter down four times and took him down twice and almost had him counted out. The fighters around me jumped up and screamed, "What did you do to that marine?" Unfortunately, he lost the second and third rounds, as the fighter tied him up repeatedly. He did get a large bonus as best fighter of the tournament even though he lost the match.

During my sixteen years in NASCAR and open-wheel competition, I fell in love with one particular track—the Virginia International Raceway. Situated in remote Virginia hills among thickly wooded tall fir trees, it was incredibly peaceful. I told myself if I were rich, I would be driving open-wheel cars here.

It was a practice session I had with a young promising twenty-year-old driver who would go on to have a three-year career in NASCAR where the use of instant focus was critical. He took a tour around the winding road course, and his lap time was 1:26. After he came in, I sensed that he was tight and squeezing the wheel. I instructed him to do his instant focus breathing, particularly as he entered the S curves, and to relax his entire body, especially his grip on the wheel (we call it the 10-2 "death grip" whereby the left hand is at the ten o'clock position and the right hand is at two o'clock position on the steering wheel). His second lap was 1:23, a shocking three-second improvement. His mechanic looked at me, swore, and said, "I stayed up all night working on the engine and aerodynamics to get tenths of a second better, and you do your 'mumbo jumbo' stuff and knock off three seconds. You make me angry," as he walked off.

I was blessed to be in Rio for the 2016 Olympics working with the U.S. Greco wrestling team. I visited with the 2012 Olympic champion of free-style wrestling, who had downloaded onto his phone my six audio files. I had worked with him previously in college, where he won a national championship. He was also voted the top Olympic American athlete in 2012. I also worked with a former collegiate linebacker who won the gold and bronze in bobsledding and later received a PhD in engineering. I'm very proud of these guys.

I developed a great relationship with a talented business leader in the finance field who wanted to get better at trapshooting. He attributed my working with him on breathing techniques to his winning a national championship. The same technique is applied by snipers and biathletes. They try to shoot between heartbeats and slowly squeeze the trigger on exhalation after slowing the heart rate.

I have been privileged to work with collegiate all-Americans, lottery picks, and NBA players. If there is one skill most important to teach them, it is to acquire the diaphragmatic breathing technique. I experimented one day in a Nebraska basketball team practice. I found that when players practice free throws, their heart rate is around 70 beats per minute. Then I asked the players to run up and down the court four times, and their heart rates jumped to 140 beats per minute—twice the rate of what they practiced. Just think of what your heart rate is when the game is on the line, at the end of the game when you are tired, and free throws can determine the outcome of the game and even a championship. As soon as a person is fouled, they have about ten seconds before they shoot the free throws. Do a couple of deep breaths to calm your body, slow your heart rate. Then breathe in while going down in your shot and breathe out while going up as you release the ball. These actions force you to relax and keep your technique and mechanics consistent. Mental precedes the physical!

WORK

A perfect example of a Top Gun performer who needed to employ instant focus skills is Chesley Burnett "Sully" Sullenberger, an American airline captain. On January 15, 2009, Sully landed US Airways flight 149 in the Hudson River off Manhattan after both engines were disabled by a bird strike. Having only seconds to make a life-saving decision, Sully calmly calculated his alternatives without enough power to circle back to the airport and being surrounded by skyscrapers. When Sully safely landed the aircraft in the river, all 155 persons aboard survived. His actions were an amazing display of staying calm and controlling his mind and body to make the only and best decision for everyone's safety. He went on to have a successful career.

The power of staying visibly calm in the midst of enormous stress occurred more than sixty years ago in 1960 in the first televised debate between U.S. presidential candidates, with Richard Nixon and John F. Kennedy. Nixon appeared on camera to be visibly nervous, sweat accumulated on his face, he fidgeted, and his eyes darted around the room. Kennedy was all smiles, calm, reassuring, and polished, using strong gestures as he stared into the camera. Interestingly, the television audiences thought Kennedy won the debate by a landslide, while radio audiences thought Nixon won by a landslide. The presidential election was one of the closest in American history. John F. Kennedy won the popular vote by the slim margin of one hundred thousand votes and all the key states in the electoral college. As a result of this election, the use of media and technology has dramatically changed performance strategies for all Top Gun performers. It is how you look and act as much as or more than what you say.

I treated a talented actor who presented with stage fright. Symptoms present as an instant panic attack after being calm until you stand in front of a camera or a live audience and then freeze. The standard treatment for decades and still used today is to take a beta-blocker medication to slow the heart rate. It is a fairly rapid-acting medication, but it can have some side effects. By utilizing the instant relaxation–instant focus techniques, he was able to correct this emotional reaction after three months of practice.

A colleague of mine is a psychologist in California. He was using a chain saw to clear deadwood from his acreage when a tree fell the wrong way and he received a glancing blow to the head. Bleeding profusely, he arrived at the ER with elevated blood pressure, heart rate, and respirations, and the surgeon was worried about having him go into shock. All of a sudden, his vitals started to slow, dropping dramatically to almost normal. The surgeon said, "Whoa, what is happening?" My friend, who practiced meditation and breathing exercises, said, "Oh, nothing to worry about, Doc, I am just doing my relaxation exercises." The physician said, "Well, whatever you are doing just keep it up!" The power of the mind to change our physiology is huge.

I was asked to provide treatment for a forty-five-year-old general surgeon who practiced in a rural community. He was the only surgeon in a fairly large area. In our early sessions he shared that he had a severe fear of failure. "What if I get inside a patient's belly and I freeze and I can't get out?" I have treated a number of physicians, especially surgeons, who carry visual images of patients who died, and they question themselves about what they could have done differently under some highly stressful situations. I specifically recall an ex-NFL player who graduated from Harvard and was a successful surgeon. He shared with me how helpful the audio files were for his football performance, but he also listened to the instant focus audio file before complex surgeries lasting four to eight hours during which he practiced his breathing exercises.

7

Self-Talks +/− in the Zone

The inner speech, your thoughts, can cause you to be rich or poor, loved or
unloved, happy or unhappy, attractive or unattractive, powerful or weak.
—RALPH CHARELL

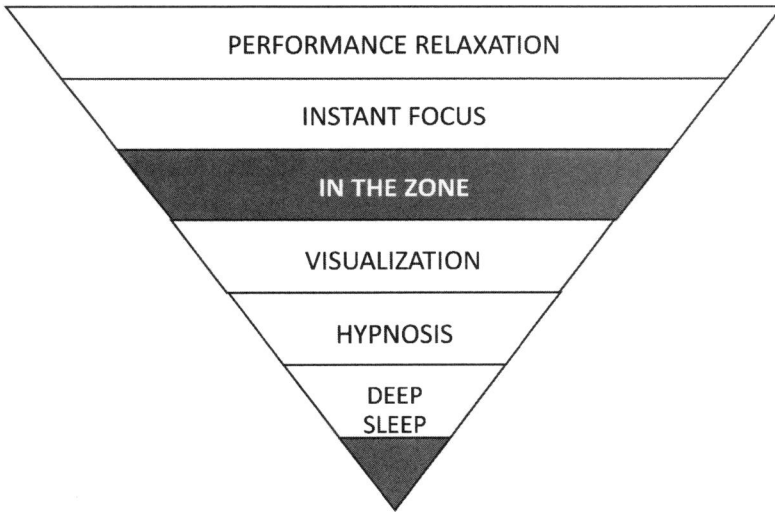

Fig. 15. Performance enhancement skills: In the zone. Created by Jack Stark.

We have been blessed to work with some of the most impressive Top Gun
performers in the world—from world leaders, high-ranking politicians, gifted
military leaders, billionaires, and Fortune 500 CEOs to all-American athletes,
Olympic gold medal winners, lottery picks, first-round picks, and national
athletes of the year.

The characteristic that never ceases to amaze us is the number of superstars
in all occupations who—although they may hide it—struggle with low self-

esteem, battle for self-confidence, and engage in negative self-talks. They can be hard on themselves in their drive to be perfect.

Recently I attended an award presentation for an extremely impressive seventeen-year-old high school senior who shared her story. She had almost a perfect score on the ACT college entrance exam, had two years of college credits before she entered college, had the highest academic math scores in the state, was an impressive athlete and leader, looked physically attractive, and came from a family of superstars. How could she, and millions of others, have so much going for themselves yet struggle with the psychological challenge of low self-esteem?

I attended a Horatio Alger Awards banquet where the recipients receive the second-highest civilian award (next to the Presidential Medal of Freedom) for a lifetime of achievements, particularly those who had humble beginnings (Oprah Winfrey having been a previous winner). The recipient was Ted Turner, billionaire, real-estate mogul, and creator of a media conglomerate (TNT). He shared with the audience that despite all his achievements, he still struggled with self-confidence deep down—and that was perhaps why he was so driven to be successful.

What Are Self-Talks?

Self-talks are the practice of talking or thinking either silently or aloud, mostly negatively about our feelings, emotions, and behaviors. Self-talks define us and help us to shape our behavior and the way we interpret our place in the world and interact with others. Self-talks shape what we call self-esteem, self-confidence, and self-image, which often determines success for Top Gun performers.

I stood next to a senior Division II wrestler who I had worked with for years. He was down to the last minute of the national final and got injured, barely losing to the reigning national champion.

After graduation he channeled the disappointment of that loss into competing in triathlons. He had a big national event coming up and asked for my help.

While working with elite athletes in running events, I often ran with them to diagnose any flaws that would hold them back from a championship performance. The technique I used was to try to get "inside their body" to feel their tension, pain, and pace.

I noticed with this triathlete that he clenched his hands, was a bit stiff, and seemed intensely focused. I asked him to relax his body (audio file 1); slow his breathing (audio file 2) by becoming more rhythmic; alter his negative self-talks about his aching leg (audio file 3); visualize a large tree two miles ahead (audio file 4); and use hypnosis (audio file 5) an hour before the race and the sleep audio file (audio file 6) the two nights before his next race.

What happened? Well, in his next race he posted his best personal time ever.

It is interesting that this experience also helped him to be a better head coach at a private high school where the team won twelve straight state championships during his tenure.

Cause of Self-Talks

We know from lots of research that positive or negative self-talks have a huge impact on performance. This internal dialogue involving both the conscious and subconscious parts of our mind is caused by both nurture (our childhood and past experiences) and nature (our genetic inheritance).

Any discussion on the nature-versus-nurture component of our health and behavior is always difficult due to the complex continuous interaction of these two determiners of human traits. Some behaviors have a slightly more genetic influence—introversion, pessimism—than self-talks, which are primarily impacted by childhood experiences reinforced through experiences in adolescence and adulthood. Parents, teachers, coaches, peers, and now social media all impact the critical thought process that impacts our behavior and performance.

Impact of Stress on Our Lives

Top Gun performers often ask, "What is the cause of all the problems we see in the world?" Perhaps we are the "hammer," and the solutions look like the "nail" approach, but mental illness (as described earlier) and the incredibly high levels of stress we experience in the world today are major sources of our worries.

The environment, war, economy, jobs, family, health, et cetera: there are lots of things to worry about. Thirty years ago, we used to make presentations on stress. The same concepts apply today, only our stress levels have significantly increased and the causes are more complex yet better understood from a research level.

I could pull out the old same black-and-white slides about stress that I used in presentations some forty years ago, and many would be relevant today.

Stress was first studied by the "godfather" of the stress field, Hans Selye. I remember his lab experiments with two groups of lab rats. One group was exposed to noise, crowding, and limited food. The results included ulcerated sores in their stomachs, bloated adrenal glands, and hearts of "stone" from all the stress.

The American Institute of Stress aptly points out that no definition of stress is accepted by everyone. Indeed, it impacts each of us differently—some not at all, while others can be debilitated.

For most of us, stress causes negative feelings and emotions. These negative feelings and emotions have a big and even bigger impact on Top Gun performers.

Our lives are impacted by minor changes: one second, one inch, one wrong tweet, or a slipup in a presentation. One wrong move in a fighter jet can have lifelong implications.

A Model of Levels of Stress

The model in figure 16 shows that if we are calm or even bored, our level of stress is low but so is our level of performance. Yet when we have good stress (eustress), our performance can peak, but too much bad stress (distress) can significantly decrease performance.

From the previous model, the discussion on "good stress" producing a good performance is true—like winning a race, scoring a big corporate merger, completing a successful but dangerous mission, or winning an election—but few discuss the side effects: the emotional, mental, and physical toll.

Perhaps that is why we have so much burnout at an early age among gifted Top Gun performers who walk away from a promising career.

We hear far too many talented people say that running for office or taking a top leadership role in a company requiring frequent moving or time away from their families is simply not worth it.

Types of Stress (American Psychiatric Association)
  1. Acute. The most common type of stress occurs from the pressures of the recent past and anticipated demands of the near future. It's a

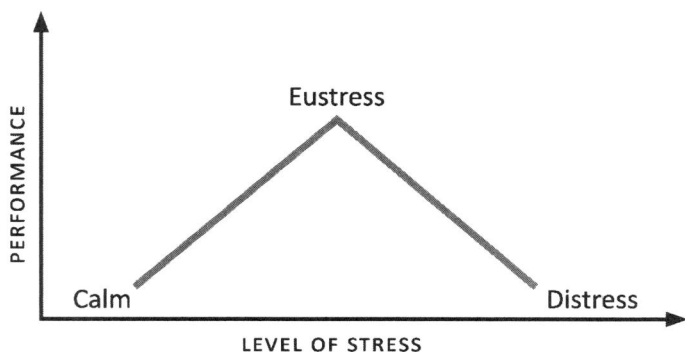

Fig. 16. Performance and level of stress. Created by Jack Stark.

missed deadline, failed contract, sick child at home. In small doses, acute stress is expected, but too much of it can lead to anger, anxiety, tension headache, jaw pain, and digestive problems.

2. Episodic acute. When acute stress builds up, migraines, hypertension, chest pain, and other more serious symptoms can occur. Pockets of life become disordered, and chaos ensues—you're always rushing, and you become aggressive, impatient, harried, or hostile.

3. Chronic. This is grinding stress that goes on for months or years. It can be the stress of poverty, a dysfunctional family, an unhappy marriage, or a despised job. It can also stem from an early traumatic event that has not been dealt with. Chronic stress can lead to heart attack, stroke, and death.

Stress-related conditions contribute to 75–90 percent of all visits to health care providers in the United States.

Doctors and pills contribute only 20–30 percent to resolving chronic conditions. That means 70–80 percent of restoring a person's health is in their own hands.

Stress Statistics

From the American Psychological Association and American Institute of Stress. This will get your attention!

Top Causes of Stress in the United States

1. Job pressure
2. Money
3. Health
4. Relationships
5. Poor nutrition
6. Media overload
7. Sleep deprivation

U.S. Stress Statistics

1. Percentage of people who regularly experience physical symptoms caused by stress	77%
2. Percentage who cite money or work as the leading cause of their stress	76%
3. Percentage who regularly experience psychological symptoms caused by stress	73%
4. Percentage who feel their stress has increased over the past five years	48%
5. Percentage who report lying awake at night due to stress	48%
6. Percentage who feel they are living with extreme stress	33%

Stress Impact Statistics

1. Percentage who say stress has caused them to fight with people close to them	54%
2. Percentage who say stress has a negative impact on their personal and professional life	48%
3. Percentage who cite jobs interfering with family or personal time as a significant source of stress	35%
4. Employed adults who say they have difficulty managing work and family responsibilities	31%

5. Percentage who report being alienated from a friend or family member because of stress	26%
6. Annual costs to employers in stress-related health care and missed work	$300 billion

People Who Cite Physical Symptoms Experience the Following

1. Fatigue	51%
2. Headache	44%
3. Upset stomach	34%
4. Muscle tension	30%
5. Change in appetite	23%
6. Teeth grinding	17%
7. Change in sex drive	15%
8. Feeling dizzy	13%

People Who Cite Psychological Symptoms Experience the Following

1. Irritability or anger	50%
2. Feeling nervous	45%
3. Lack of energy	45%
4. Feeling as though you could cry	35%

Treating Stress Disorders

In the early 1980s I had a difficult choice to make. I was offered a job as the first and only medical psychologist for a large clinic of physicians. This group grew from thirty to two hundred physicians ranging from primary care to every surgery and specialty care available.

I decided to leave the university medical center as a tenured professor in the departments of psychiatry and pediatrics to join this group. At the time I had no real idea that this model of being embedded in the internal medicine department would be the model of choice today.

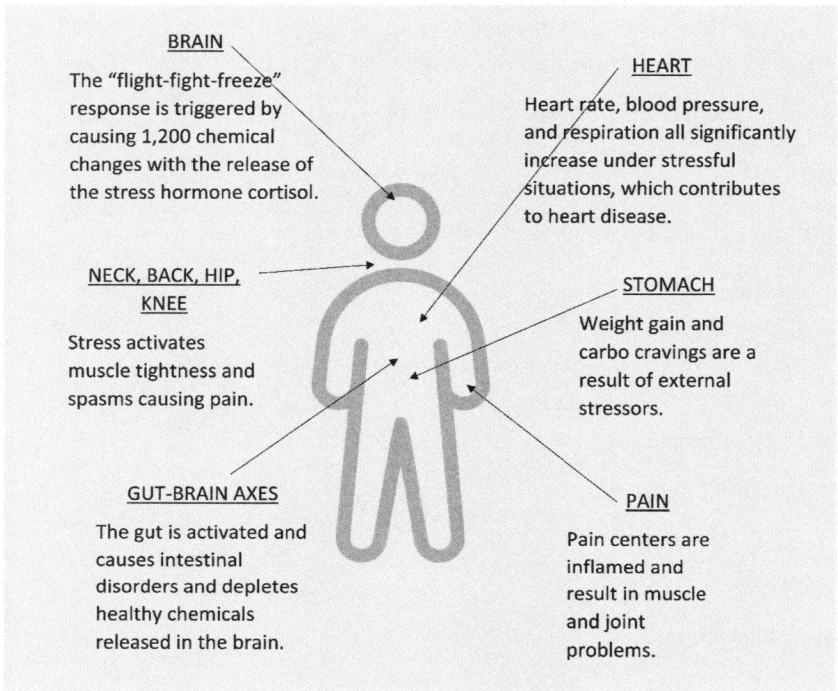

BRAIN
The "flight-fight-freeze" response is triggered by causing 1,200 chemical changes with the release of the stress hormone cortisol.

HEART
Heart rate, blood pressure, and respiration all significantly increase under stressful situations, which contributes to heart disease.

NECK, BACK, HIP, KNEE
Stress activates muscle tightness and spasms causing pain.

STOMACH
Weight gain and carbo cravings are a result of external stressors.

GUT-BRAIN AXES
The gut is activated and causes intestinal disorders and depletes healthy chemicals released in the brain.

PAIN
Pain centers are inflamed and result in muscle and joint problems.

Fig. 17. Stress and your body: Stress affects the entire body. Created by Jack Stark.

Instead of sending patients across town to see the "shrink" with all its negative connotations, they could send individuals down the hall to see me. For the next thirty years I was able to see ten thousand patients and was referred to top business leaders, to professionals in medicine, law, and politics, and eventually to sports teams.

I explained to the medical group what I could offer. After one year the group made me the only non-MD full partner—a tribute to the model versus the person.

I wanted to lower medication use or eliminate it in some cases and change the delivery of medical care so the docs could work with the more complicated cases requiring surgery or intensive treatment.

My primary focus was on stress. Thus, I ran a biofeedback practice treating physical disorders—high blood pressure, headaches, pain, irritable bowel syndrome, insomnia, and almost every imaginable physical ailment.

In addition, I provided individual and couple therapy. I tried to offer a third type of medicine—behavior medicine.

Their approach to medicine then was (1) to do surgery, (2) to prescribe medication, or (3) to refer for treatment of lifestyle issues. Certainly, these were necessary treatments for many individuals. Others, however, exhibited behavioral problems that either made their medical condition worse or were best treated by a medical psychologist or an allied health professional.

In addition to this challenge, I was booked for months. In short, I had to devise a method of helping my patients, athletes, and Top Gun performers develop self-control by giving my skills away to them. As a result, I came up with the development of audio files designed to treat specific behavioral problems.

Audio file 1: Performance Relaxation—stress and anxiety.

Audio file 2: Instant Focus—breathing for performance and panic attacks.

Audio file 3: Self-Talks—depression and physical ailments.

Audio file 4: Visualization—overcoming fears and improving performance.

Audio file 5: Hypnosis—for trauma and competition.

Audio file 6: Deep Sleep—for treating insomnia to prevent anxiety, depression, and more serious psychological disorders.

In the forty years of using these audio files (revised many times) with the instructions contained in each chapter of this book, I have been overwhelmed with the result on patients and athletes, particularly Top Gun performers.

I have received thousands of emails, texts, cards, and so forth telling me how they benefited from the audio files and talks, which helped to produce state championships, national championships, Olympic medals, and most of all significant increase in self-esteem and confidence.

POSITIVE SELF-TALKS

Recently I had a collegiate volleyball player tell me how much the mental-performance training and audio files were helping her. Then she introduced me to her mother, who told me I had treated a team she had been on, which made it to the final four in volleyball and had listened to the hypnosis audio file before the championship games thirty years ago!

STRESS REDUCTION

Reducing stress is a national priority. Directly in medical costs and indirectly in lost productivity, stress costs our country hundreds of billions of dollars each year.

People ask why mental illness is growing, and I answer—*stress*. The mental and physical toll is now better understood, but all treatment systems are overwhelmed.

One day I was standing in the hallway outside my office in the internal medicine department I shared with the three physicians. I looked down the hall at Dr. Jim, who walked out of one room, picked up the chart to see the next patient, and yelled down the hall, "Dr. Stark, I saw fifty patients today and forty-eight needed to see you!" Message received.

Today people cope via exercise, yoga, meditation, listening to music, and mindfulness. I have attended workshops on mindfulness and each time left confused. It is less a treatment process than it is a label for shutting the mind off. Simply put, mindfulness—being "full of your mind," not thinking of the past or future and blocking out all distractions—is getting "in the zone." I first borrowed this concept from those who practiced Buddhism and used various types of meditation. Perhaps meditation, relaxation, training, reflective prayer, and similar activities contain religious connotations, so "mindfulness" becomes a popular word summarizing a movement to combat stress.

Using each of the audio files was originally designed for my patients, but I soon discovered they were even more effective with elite athletes and high performers in the business world.

Levels of Self-Talk

In my opinion there is a direct correlation between the increasing stress level in our lives and the toll it takes on our daily performance—physically, mentally, and emotionally.

Technology brings unimaginable benefits to our lives but at some cost personally unless we control our worries. Life was stressful during the past two centuries, but the pace was slower, with quiet time to reflect without

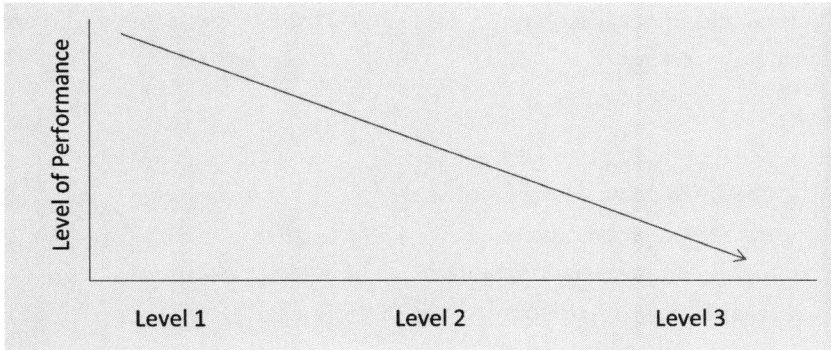

Fig. 18. The three levels of self-talks. Created by Jack Stark.

being bombarded by messages of doom on TV, radio, phone calls, email, and social media.

It occurs to me from a psychological perspective that there are two types of people in this world: (1) those of us who have made it and are afraid we will lose it, and (2) those of us who have not made it and are afraid that we never will make it. Both types are burdened with excessive worries.

Being bombarded with worry messages reminds us we can lose it all or never reach our goals.

The Three Levels of Self-Talks

Level 1: Mildly negative self-talks lead to *anxiety*.

Level 2: Mildly to moderately negative self-talks lead to *depression*.

Level 3: Moderately to severely negative self-talks lead to obsessive rumi-nating, *loss of focus*, and more severe forms of anxiety, depression, and physical symptoms.

The number one reason in my experience, by far, that Top Gun performers seek professionals' assistance, whether in school, sports, or work, is the negative self-talks they engage in daily.

Causes of Negative Self-Talks

Why do we talk negatively to ourselves? My experience is that individuals today are constantly evaluated either by themselves or by others. There are internal and external scorecards, particularly for elite performers who are constantly scrutinized.

The profile we often see is

1. perfectionistic personalities,
2. a desire to do well from an early age,
3. wanting to please others,
4. highly competitive,
5. talented academically, athletically, and socially,
6. leadership characteristics,
7. morally and ethically well-grounded,
8. highly disciplined,
9. goal-oriented—achievement-directed, and
10. wanting never to let others down or let themselves down—high expectations.

This psychological profile is a blessing if one can control the negative self-talks.

Process of Negative Self-Talks

Level 1: The Top Gun performer wakes up in the morning and soon starts to think about the negative information they are bombarded with. This negativity creates a loop in their mind whereby their thinking all morning leads to increased anxiety.

Level 2: If the Top Gun performer cannot get out of this worry loop of negative thinking, then by noon one can begin to experience symptoms of depression—lack of focus, poor decision-making, fatigue, withdrawal, and sadness, among others.

Level 3: As the self-talks increase in severity, duration, and frequency, they can lead to obsessive rumination, which sends signals of significant stress to your body.

The negative self-talk process of a looping system that we can't turn off sucks all the energy out of us and greatly impacts our performance.

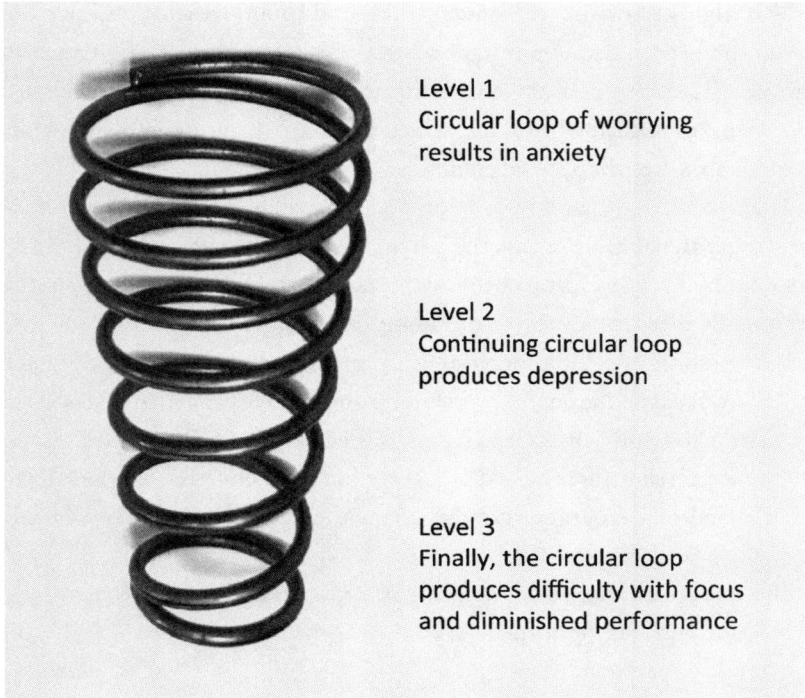

Level 1
Circular loop of worrying
results in anxiety

Level 2
Continuing circular loop
produces depression

Level 3
Finally, the circular loop
produces difficulty with focus
and diminished performance

Fig. 19. Faulty thinking. Created by Jack Stark.

The Psychophysiology of Negative Self-Talks

Everyone has heard of the fight-flight-freeze response. Our bodies have highly evolved since the Stone Age, when our main defense mechanism for survival was to have this built-in reaction process in our body. Think of it like a car with a nitro button or a jet with an afterburner, used to fight a saber-toothed tiger or to give someone the energy to run. If one becomes too scared, however, we can freeze.

This psychological (mind)–physiological (body) process takes place instantaneously. When a threat is perceived, the signal is processed in our mind and sent to our energy button to squirt into our bloodstream chemicals to help us react. Within one-tenth of a second our body has more than a thousand chemical reactions.

This highly sophisticated system is referred to in medicine and psychology as the hypothalamic-pituitary-adrenal axis (HPA axis). This HPA axis of our central stress response system is characterized by hypothalamic release of corticotropin-releasing hormone, which binds to the pituitary gland, which in turn stimulates the adrenal glands.

The two adrenal glands have an on-and-off switch. As soon as they receive the danger signal, they release the adrenaline (cortisol) and whamo! We are wired for hours. These alarm chemicals, if activated too often, however, produce stress levels that are harmful to our bodies and our performance.

It is a bit like riding a motorcycle. When the engine is in idle, then all is quiet and relaxed. When the engine is revved up, more energy is demanded—which is what we do to ourselves when we get revved up inside. The problem is, not everyone can tell we are stressed out, as we can carry our stress around all day, stuck in neutral gear yet constantly revving the motor but going nowhere by engaging in negative self-talks.

The impact on our body—heart, gut, brain, and muscular system—can greatly diminish our performance.

Obsessive Thinking

Obsessive thinking is a serious problem. Obsessive thinking is an inability to gain control over recurrent, distressing thoughts or images. This process can be mildly distracting to totally debilitating. You cannot remove it by surgery or take a pill to alleviate symptoms, as it is more in the mind than in the brain and is a bad habit best controlled with cognitive behavioral techniques.

Behavior therapy became the go-to therapy in the 1960s and 1970s, but it soon became known that our thoughts—thinking or cognitive component—also needed to be changed along with our behavior.

Since the 1980s cognitive behavioral techniques (used throughout these chapters and the audio files) have become the gold standard of all therapies and are as powerful as medication for some individuals with mild to moderate psychological disorders. (Research on psychotherapy often compares ten sessions to some medications as being equally effective.)

Hypothalamus

Pituitary Gland

Adrenal Cortex

ADRENALINE
External events trigger activation of the hypothalamus, which signals the pituitary to stimulate the adrenal glands, which instantly secrete the stress hormones adrenaline and cortisol.

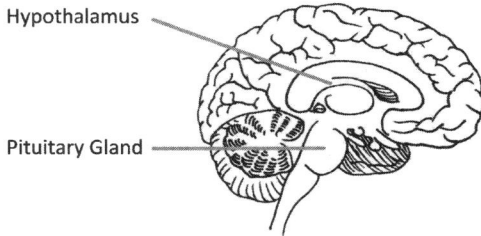

Fig. 20. Adrenaline and the body. Created by Jack Stark.

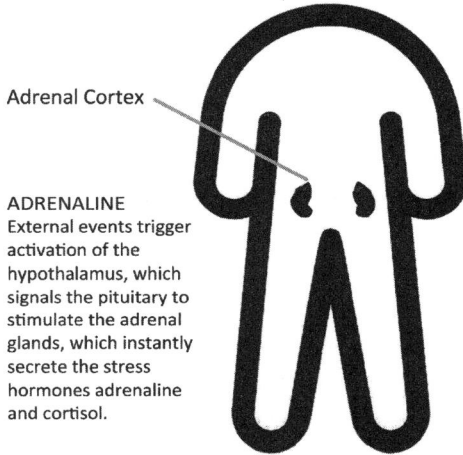

An athlete's obsessive thinking while eating or standing in line for food:

"The steak looks good; this is a big game. Maybe I will eat some vegetables. Hope I don't blow it. Dessert – not today. Everyone is counting on me."

Fig. 21. Obsessive thinking. Created by Jack Stark.

Types of Negative Self-Talks

We are often asked, "Why does [my son, daughter, spouse, player, CEO, or highly respected leader] engage in this phenomenon we label 'negative self-talks'?" In the past few years especially, the request for consultation particularly to high school and college Top Gun performers is due to this pattern of negative self-talks.

Our personalities and thought patterns are shaped by our family, culture, and peers while we are growing up. Parents often feel guilty that they somehow "caused" this behavior. This is not always the case.

We tend to be shaped by many factors and often just by observation of our primary and extended family members who work hard and serve as role models. We see this behavior and want to emulate it as we see how such behavior makes those around us so successful.

It is our experience that negative self-talks tend to cluster in five distinct thinking patterns.

Selective thinking. We want to be perfect! When we get nine positive comments and one negative one, our perfectionistic style is to brush off any positive comments and allow the one negative to cancel out all the good. We hate to fail or lose more than we want to succeed and win, and we really love to win.

The gifted surgeon, the talented trial lawyers, the articulate keynote speaker, the experienced pilot, and the NBA superstar all realize that all the good they do can be erased instantly by one major slipup. Once they have experienced this negative experience, it can be hard to erase it and let go in our minds.

Either/or thinking. Either/or thinking can take a toll on our bodies via this view of the world and our silent self-communication. We tend to divide everything into good or bad thoughts and focus on the bad, especially when it comes to making everyone around us happy. The difficulty with this *distorted thinking* is making everyone else happy all the time. We think there is no middle ground and tend to blame ourselves, wallowing in our perceived failure. Sometimes those around us can even consciously or subconsciously reinforce this behavior to have their own needs better met or to get the attention they crave.

Why does this happen? There is a great deal of anger in the world, and it seems to be growing. There is much that divides people—the haves and the have-nots. You have something I want, and it is not fair that I have less, so give me some of what you have. There are others who struggle in life for many reasons and project their anger on you if you are successful.

There is a common phenomenon in therapy. When a patient projects certain negative emotions onto the therapist, the therapist, who learns during training that this can happen, particularly early in therapy, is reminded not to have "countertransference" whereby the therapist transfers that hurt or anger back onto the patient, client, or Top Gun performer.

Over the years, individuals who have gone through this process of transference to me, many times because they have been hurt, disappointed in a loss, or sustained a setback, later seek to apologize. I explain they never have to apologize—although it is appreciated—because if I can't understand and accept this interaction, then I should not be in the performance business.

Some individuals may be experiencing a midlife crisis, and you, as their therapist, are shocked by their behavior as you have never seen it before and wonder what you did wrong.

There is also a smaller group of individuals who you thought you perhaps knew well but find out they are toxic, manipulative, and craving money and power.

For those in the "helping" profession, remember to keep things in perspective and be careful not to blame yourself or to have difficulty letting go.

Disaster thinking. Disaster thinking is expecting a disaster to happen and engaging in self-defeating thinking patterns that can bring about the very behavior we are trying to avoid.

Fairness thinking. We expect life to be fair. When we help others, we expect it will be appreciated and that we will be thanked for it. When this outcome does not occur, we become upset and dwell on why.

Reward thinking. We can get locked into thinking that all our hard work and sacrifice will pay off as if someone were keeping score. "Why is this happening to me? After all, look at all the good that I do for others. Life is not fair. I should be rewarded for my behavior, and I am terribly disappointed that this is not happening. I can't shut my mind off on this type of negative thinking."

Monitoring Self-Talks

One of the most effective ways of reducing negative self-talks is to measure the frequency of our engagement in this process. I have utilized the "behav-

30% of the people you help will be angry at you for helping them. This is hard to accept. Their behavior is often due to their circumstances in life, and they project their disappointment onto you.

30% of the people may appreciate your help but you will never hear from them—they are absorbed with their daily life challenges.

30% The last thirty percent will not only appreciate what you did for them, but they will let you know—calls, thank-you notes, personal comments to you and others—and remember what you did for them for life.

10% This group will not only appreciate your help, let you know about it, and tell everyone else, but they also become lifelong friends and make it all worthwhile.

Fig. 22. Remember the 30-30-30 rule. Created by Jack Stark.

ioral diary" technique whereby our Top Gun performers track the number of "uppers," or positive things each day. Even little things—a comment, a look, a compliment—can affect our day. What I have found is that when people try this powerful technique of "uppers and downers" recordkeeping, there is a rapid 18 percent increase in one's positive symptoms as they get a better perspective on the ratio of good and bad, their false assumptions, and the uselessness of dwelling on just the negatives.

Why Do We Have Conflict—and Worry about It!

When one is in the helping professions or a leadership role, there is a tendency to hold ourselves accountable for all our "failures." While this habit can assist us in not repeating our mistakes, it can cause some long nights.

We have often reflected over our lifetime on when we clashed with certain individuals. What did we do wrong to have them react so negatively to us?

Here is what I discovered by composing a list of the top one hundred people I clashed with in high school and throughout my career—maybe two people a year. The results: Five of them either went to jail or experienced legal issues. Eighty-four of them were fired, demoted, put on a performance-improvement plan, or changed to lower-paying jobs. And eleven were transferred or forced into early retirement.

In short, while one recognizes their mistakes, be also aware that in your lifetime you will meet many on your life's journey who you cannot please, save, or fix and who are toxic to those they interact with. The Judas syndrome has been around for centuries.

In the Zone: Negative Self-Talks (Audio File 3)

These five faulty thinking patterns can decrease performance via our psychophysiological response to hundreds of chemical changes to our bodies in one-tenth of a second.

Imagine if we get stuck in this negative loop thinking all day, yet that is what happens to us.

To block these negative self-talks, this audio file training takes you through three steps.

1. *Imagine the thoughts.* Visually imagine the negative self-talks by putting yourself in a situation where you recall a specific instance where you could see, hear, smell, and feel your reaction and the reactions of others.

2. *Interrupt the negative talks.* Interrupt the negative self-talk by using the S.T.O.P. technique. This interrupts the looping, spinning internal conversation we have with ourselves about upsetting events—big or small. The S.T.O.P. technique is designed to break the cycle for thirty seconds and help you learn how to extend this time until you can eliminate this type of negative thinking. I often use a one-cent rubber band on the wrist and snap it or click my fingers to send a message to the brain to stop spinning. The snap stings briefly and sends a signal

up our spinal cord to the brain, and our attention is drawn to that sensation. This technique works well, as it is cheap, quick, and easy to use with none of the side effects we see in medications.

3. *Replacing the negative thoughts.* After you imagine the negative thought and interrupt it, then you need to replace it with positive self-talks that eliminate the fight-flight-freeze reaction of our bodies.

There are many ways to make this change. You can mentally go to the beach or your favorite place to relax and shut down the negative thinking.

If that does not work, then "obsess about something good," your best performances, with positive self-affirmations. "I feel great, strong, and happy." I often dwell on winning the lottery and setting up a foundation to help others. When I get done with this daydreaming, the "good feelings" replace the "yucky feelings."

How Do Negative Self-Talks Impact Performance?

Research tells us that negative automatic thoughts are precursors to the onset and recurrence of psychological symptoms of depression and anxiety (Beck 1967). Worry and rumination are highly correlated and are associated with emotions such as anxiety and depression (Ehring and Watkins 2008).

Rumination is defined as a mode of thinking that involves repetitively and passively focusing on one's symptoms or a negative event in the past. Studies have shown that rumination intensified negative mood states, enhanced negative thinking and memory, and impaired social problem solving in dysphoric individuals (Lyubomirsky and Tkach 2004).

Negative self-thoughts, self-doubting thoughts, and worrying about not doing well have been identified as common cognitive stressors (Gould, Eck-lund, and Jackson 1992; Gould, Jackson, and Finch 1993).

Researchers suggest that cognitive response to injuries can influence physical and psychological recovery. Cognition and affect are proposed to have direct and indirect relations with return to sport outcomes (Wiese-Bjornstal, Smith, Shaffer, and Morrey 1998; Brewer, Andersen, and Van Raalte 2002).

High levels of competitive anxiety are also associated with poor performance and a reduction in the enjoyment of participation. Anxiety is also an important predictor of discontinuation of sports participation (Scanlan, Babkes, and Scanlan 2005; Smith and Smoll 1991; Gould, Feltz, Horn, and Weiss 1982).

Anxiety associated with competition or performance has been identified as a major predictor of the quality and the duration of one's experiences in athletics and other achievement domains like academics and business (Gould, Greenleaf, and Krane 2002; Smith, Smoll, and Passer 2002).

A study involving semiprofessional soccer players showed that positive thought control training increased both physical and decision-making performance along with reducing anxiety (Maynard, Smith, and Warwick-Evans 1995).

"Various forms of Recurrent Negative Thoughts (RNT) have been associated with the onset, duration, severity and maintenance of depressive episodes . . . , poor problem-solving . . . , a range of encoding, memory, and emotional processing biases . . . , avoidance of negative affect . . . , and inhibition of emotional processing" (McEvoy, Moulds, and Mahoney 2014).

Repetitive negative thinking involves thinking about one or more negative topics that are experienced as hard to control (Ehring and Watkins 2008). Some forms of repetitive negative thinking, rumination, and worry were found to be positively correlated with multiple forms of psychological distress (Nolen-Hoeksema 1991).

Negative thinking is positively correlated with anxiety, depression, anger, and other psychopathologies, and is negatively correlated with life satisfaction and happiness (Wong 2012).

Worrying affects performance on a task. In a research study, subjects were asked to sort things into two categories. Participants who reported they worry 50 percent of the time or more showed a significant disruption in their ability to perform well on the task (Metzger et al. 1990).

Getting and Giving Positive Feedback

Some experiences in life you just never forget. These images and thoughts haunt you like a bad horror movie that keeps replaying over and over in your mind.

A life of reflection tells us that if you care about people, that when there is loss, it hurts deeper for those who care more deeply.

Childhood experiences, traumatic experiences, good times and bad: our mind records these images and self-talks, which bounce around in our heads and, unless we release them, can affect our health and performance.

Conclusion

This chapter covers an area (negative self-talks) for which there is no easy cure. We tell Top Gun performers you have to fight fire with fire—each negative thought needs to be identified and eliminated with the thought-stoppage techniques contained in this chapter and on audio file 3.

We need to stay focused and not allow the distracting thoughts that can suck us down to obsessive rumination and can keep us from focusing and performing at our best.

Controlling our self-talks is by far the number one health problem and challenge in America today and is especially challenging to those who are elite performers and leaders. As the saying goes, "To whom much is given, much is expected."

Top Gun performers are required to give feedback and receive criticism daily. We recommend avoiding toxic people if possible—CEOs, supervisors, coaches, relatives, peers, and others. When avoidance is not possible, use the techniques contained in this chapter to enhance performance in all areas of your life.

Interviews of Top Gun performers over the years and in various settings revealed that their responses to life are based on how they themselves were raised. One-third of interviewees told us, "You can say or do anything to me, as I am used to it. It does not bother me and sometimes motivates me."

Another third said that sometimes negative feedback bothers them and sometimes it does not depend on the situation in their life at the time.

The last third were emphatic: "I don't respond well to negative feedback of any kind. That's not the way I was raised or was coached."

Research shows that in order to change behavior, it is best to use four positives to every negative when giving or receiving feedback. When I share this wisdom with Top Gun performers in leadership positions, they at first scoff at that suggestion, as it seems way too positive. I point out the one negative if it is really personal or questions a person's integrity can hurt more than eight positives.

I also strongly recommend the sandwich approach: positive, negative in the form of question asking, and positive.

I had a top college basketball coach who was old-school in his coaching philosophy. He took out his prized seven-foot-two-inch center who was being outplayed by a future six-foot-eight-inch NBA star and Hall of Famer. When the center came out of the game, the coach yelled at him and made critical comments about his play. The player slammed his towel down and hung his head.

I proposed the sandwich approach to the coach, and he asked what it was. I said to let the player cool off first. Then make a positive statement: "You are my best player, and you have a great future in the NBA." Then ask why he was getting outplayed, as most people know the answer, and follow the player's answer with a positive comment: "Now you go back in there and push him around."

It worked, and we won a critical game. The player was drafted in the first round of the NBA.

The use of the sandwich approach, with its four-to-one positive-to-negative comments, produced a top-ten team, 26-7, the best season record in the history of the Power 5 school's basketball program. As the team psychologist working with this team some twenty-five hours a week, I found it gratifying to witness the realization of the full potential of the team, which had had a 10-18 losing season the year before this principle was introduced.

8

Visualization

Good business leaders create a vision, articulate the vision,
passionately own the vision, and relentlessly drive it to completion.
—JACK WELCH, GENERAL ELECTRIC

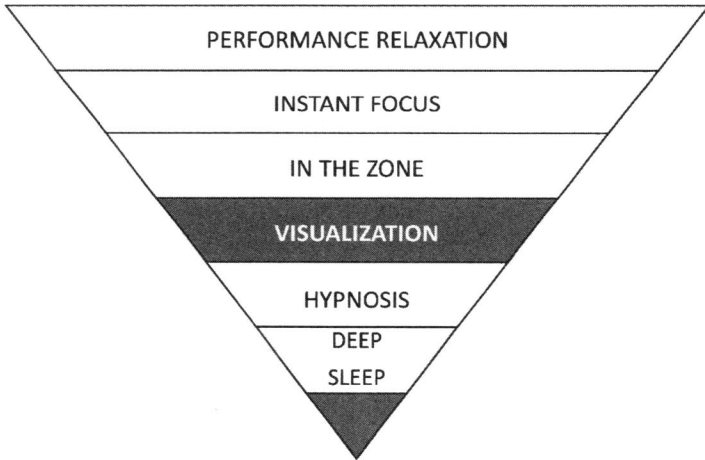

Fig. 23. Performance enhancement skills: Visualization. Created by Jack Stark.

Jack Welch was a Top Gun performer. He began his career with General Electric in 1960 and became the company's chairman in 1981. During the next twenty years he grew GE's market capitalization to more than $400 billion, making it the world's most valuable corporation.

At its height, this global conglomerate employed close to seven hundred thousand employees. But this 128-year-old company has lost 80 percent of its net worth and continues to struggle.

How? Leaders who followed Welch lacked vision.

Jack Welch in his book *Winning* outlines his mental skills, particularly his vision of what a company should be and how to best guide it in the right direction with constant improvements. GE under Welch's guidance trained hundreds of top visionary leaders to become CEO Top Gun performers in numerous Fortune 500 companies. Drawing on the management concepts of the godfather of management, Peter Drucker (*The Essential Drucker: The Best of Sixty Years of Peter Drucker's Essential Writings on Management*), and the Japanese philosophy of leadership, Welch influenced major corporations all over the world in their hiring, training, and management of companies.

Welch was particularly known for eliminating the bottom 10 percent of his company each year. He focused on training top executives, many of whom went on to be successful CEOs of more than fifty Fortune 500 companies.

Continuous Improvement Vision

Top Gun performers in their work are gifted visualizers who can paint visual pictures that others readily understand and follow in setting and attaining goals.

Many Top Gun performers have been influenced by the Japanese philosophy of *Kaizen* (*kai* meaning "to change" and *zen* meaning "good"). They focus on continuous improvement through in-depth sessions to assess employees' progress.

Companies that lack visual Top Gun performers can quickly fall behind.

Sears is a perfect example. Declaring bankruptcy in 2019, this 137-year-old venerable company was once the number one retailer in the world and was the Amazon of its day with its popular worldwide catalog business.

Perhaps an example of Top Gun performers in the work area with a vision is Uber. Uber has gone public and is valued at $150 billion, more than the values of Ford Motor Company, General Motors, and Fiat-Chrysler *combined*. Who could have envisioned this happening to hundred-year-old companies being replaced by startups with dreams?

Perhaps the greatest visualizer of the past one hundred years is Albert Einstein. "Imagination is more important than knowledge" is one of his greatest quotations.

Einstein also stated, "No problem can be solved from the same level of consciousness that created it." His ability to "see" the universe and its complex mathematical formulae distinguishes him from all other thinkers of the twentieth and twenty-first centuries.

I had an occasion in 1978 to spend a day with the second-greatest visualizer (in my opinion) and Top Gun performer in the past hundred years to have a huge impact on the world—B. F. Skinner. The Harvard psychologist was the first person to develop the science of human behavior, and both he and Einstein continue to shape our understanding of the world today.

I asked Dr. Skinner in 1978 if he was frustrated, as his book was first published in 1953 but twenty-five years later people were still trying to understand his concepts. His answer surprised me. He said that twenty-five years is not enough time to fully understand such a complex breakthrough. "Look at Einstein," he said. "It's been fifty years and we still don't understand his complex theories."

Skinner was a huge fan of Einstein and shared with me that the Hubble space telescope, and now the Webb space telescope, would help confirm a few of the great theories of Einstein. And it has taken seventy-plus years since Skinner's 1953 book *Science and Human Behavior* to better understand human behavior.

Causes of Exceptional Visual Skills

How did Einstein, at the age of twenty-six, develop his theory of relativity? After all, he was an average student in grammar school, and it was only later, on his own time, that he developed his most influential theories—via his imagination and almost childlike sense of wonder and curiosity.

Certainly, he had exceptional skills in math and science from an early age. But it was mainly his drive to see the world in a different way. This is a lesson for those who wish to develop this critical skill to improve one's performance in multiple settings.

Other twenty-first-century visualizers:

Steve Jobs at Apple,
Bill Gates at Microsoft,
Jeff Bezos at Amazon,
Sergey Brin and Larry Page at Google.

All of these Top Gun performers share one common trait that has produced four of the largest and most impactful companies in the world—their ability to visualize what could be.

What Is Visualization?

Visualization, a psychological concept for increasing performance particularly for elite athletes and leaders, was introduced in the mid-1980s by psychologist Richard Suinn (*Seven Steps to Peak Performance*, 1986). It is a powerful tool to program one's mind and body for that extra edge.

The formation of mental visual images involves focusing on positive mental images in order to achieve a particular goal or create a desired direction and understanding. History reveals all great thinkers and strategists from Socrates to Einstein engaged in this type of thinking. The truly great Top Gun performers have always used visualization through visual imagery as an effective way to communicate both abstract and concrete ideas.

Visualization is sometimes referred to as imagery or mental rehearsal. It involves cognitively creating a new experience or recreating a past experience to either practice a specific sport skill or to prepare immediately before competition. Visual imagery helps individuals understand the significance of data by placing it in a visual context.

Why Is Visualization So Important?

Because of the way our mind processes information, we can better understand and explain to others the mental picture in our minds so that everyone can "see" how they can best behave to achieve that desired peak performance.

Top Gun performers who imagine themselves performing a task improve their performance in that task. Everyone is looking for that extra edge. We often emphasize that that half-second difference in sports can be huge or that 5 percent difference in performance adds to the bottom line of a company.

Most of us are not aware of how powerful visualization can be in our lives. While almost all of us visualize daily, our brain is programmed to protect us from bad "fight or flight" situations that often pop into our minds.

Research by psychologists at the Cleveland Clinic Foundation found *that just by visualizing a task, one can improve performance without actually performing the task*. For example, a research project showed that a group of athletes who did a virtual workout over three months in their minds had a 13 percent increase in performance versus another group who actually increased muscle strength by 30 percent from their actual intense physical workout. Think about the impact of this finding. In the preseasons you can get a huge boost over your competitors by visually practicing picturing your sport. Some of the world's top golfers credit this process to their early season success before they ever pick up a club.

For many years we have used visualization techniques to treat injuries in Top Gun performers. Their injury prevents them from participating in their sport, work, or studies. If you store these visualization memories in the visual regions of your brain, it is much easier to resume your performance at a higher level by mentally practicing the visualization process.

Visualize this: think of your subconscious mind as having pathways that are activated over and over the more you visualize a certain behavior. Then when you go to perform that behavior, it is easier and faster to go down that pathway, which gives you an edge in speed and clarity to a desired outcome. This process activates the 18 billion brain cells and channels them into a purposeful direction.

Performance and Visualization

In the early 1980s, I was asked to write an essay for an issue of an orthopedic journal about the young female athlete's performance.

I was shocked by the number of requests for a copy of the chapter, a common courtesy among academic professionals. Of all the publications—articles, chapters, and books—I have written, it was by far my most requested publication, though it did not seem to warrant that kind of response.

At first, I thought it was because the focus was on the young female athlete, an area that still lacks significant research, but the requests came from Russia and many Eastern European countries. Then it dawned on me—Russia and Pavlovian conditioning! Remember the meat-bell-salivation experiment? This classic study by the Russian Pavlov involved experiments with dogs. It was referred to as a "conditioning experiment" whereby animals and people could be trained or conditioned to react a certain way. Pavlov would present a piece of meat, paired with a bell ringing, and the animal would salivate. After a while, just the bell would produce salivation in the dog—a conditioned response.

In the 1980s Russia and many other countries did not have the training facilities, diet, strength, and conditioning advantages that the United States had, but they had psychology, a powerful tool with few costs. They understood psychological principles that were cheap, easy to use, and effective at increasing performance. Soon the rest of the world took notice and began to adopt mental training tactics particularly at an early age for Olympic performances from smaller countries. They were looking for a mental edge, since they lacked the physical edge in performance.

Research Findings on Visualizations and Performance

Research has shown that mental simulation done by visualization enhances one's ability to visualize outcomes, thus increasing goal achievement (Pham and Taylor 1999). Imagery, or visualization, is widely regarded as a valuable performance engagement technique for use with athletes (Driskell, Copper, and Moran 1994).

Visualization has been shown to improve skills such as self-confidence, self-efficacy, motivation, and managing competitive anxiety (Slimani et al. 2016). It also affects performance by helping modify the mental representations of action, thus improving the athletes' expertise levels (Land, Frank, and Schack 2014; Ericsson and Ward 2007).

Using imagery can also aid in healing sports injuries. Visualization that incorporates breathing exercises helps reduce muscle tension, which is associated with increased pain and inhibited healing (Dworsky and Krane n.d.).

Just *imagining* yourself performing a sports skill causes EMG (electromyographic) activity in the musculature resembling that which would occur during the actual physical execution of the skill. The EMG pattern is not completely identical, but the neural impulses passed from the brain to the muscular system during the imagery can be retained in memory as if the movement had actually happened (Schmidt et al. 2017).

When, Where, and How to Use Visualization Training: Audio File 4

The more frequently one practices their visualization training, the more quickly and effectively they can draw on this skill to maximize their performance for almost any occasion.

When we go to the mountains, we are often struck by the quiet solitude of nature versus the level of auditory and visual stimulation that bombards us daily in cities. The stress of our lives tends to keep us in a state of constant "fight or flight" mode with racing thoughts and diminished visualization skills.

We sometimes need to find a quiet place to shut off all outside distraction. Doing so allows for more vividly seeing ourselves in a situation, particularly just before competition or during the week in preparation for the critical event.

Success depends on a positive image in your mind. The opposite is also true; if you think and "see" yourself failing, the odds are that you will indeed underperform.

STEPS TO USING AUDIO FILE 4

This ten-minute audio file takes you through five progressive steps in which mental imagery is rehearsed and thus is embedded in your mind to produce a powerful skill for Top Gun performers.

Step 1: Body Scan. People fail to realize the amount of tension and often pain stored in the musculoskeletal system. By quietly scanning each part of your body starting at the top of your head all the way to your feet, you can identify the amount and location of tension and reduce it by letting go of the musculoskeletal tension.

Step 2: Relaxation Breathing. Deep relaxation breathing (see chapter 5) slows the heart rate, drops blood pressure, and calms the mind. This breathing tells the vagus nerve to signal a calming effect and block any upsetting thoughts via support to the parasympathetic nervous system, the nervous system that relaxes the body.

Step 3: Progressive Muscle Relaxation. Progressive muscle relaxation is a muscle-relaxation technique that has been used in clinical and nonclinical settings for decades. It involves learning to monitor the tension in specific muscle groups based on the premise that muscle tension is the body's psychological response to anxiety-producing thoughts that can be blocked. It was first introduced by Harvard physician Edmund Jacobsen in 1929. It involves a tightening of muscles followed by a release of the muscles to feel the difference and help one to tune into their muscle tension throughout the entire body in a progressive tightening-releasing process. In this step we abbreviate the process to simply focus and identify the muscle tension throughout the body and relax specific muscle groups. Letting go of muscle-tension stored in the body, particularly the neck and shoulders area, is essential to maximizing the visualization process.

Step 4: Sensory Awareness. We are rarely aware of using each of our senses to tune into the world around us. Visualizing a forest, practicing using our senses of *hearing, seeing, smelling, and touching,* can train our mind to tune into sensory input and help us to better visualize.

Step 5: Visualize Your Best Performance. Our brain is programmed to protect us via life experiences—particularly the danger of failure. Too often our minds drift to "what not to do." (See chapter 7, about negative self-talks and images.) By seeing your best performance in school, sports, or work in preparation for competition, you now have a blueprint of how to perform faster and better.

The Power of Visualization

We occasionally hear stories of incredible mental and physical feats shared by individuals who have endured unimaginable torture and survival.

Our protective minds react by questioning if such human behavior is even possible. A well-documented experience of a seven-year prisoner of war in Vietnam is exemplary of the power of visualization.

James Nesmeth was a pilot who was shot down over Vietnam and captured. He spent seven years imprisoned in a cage that was four and a half feet long and five feet tall. Let that sink in!

Your reaction may be like mine when I first heard this story: "How could anyone survive this kind of torture—mentally, physically, and spiritually?"

During his time of imprisonment, Nesmeth saw only guards and talked to no one. At first, he prayed and hoped he would soon be released. He quickly realized, however, that he would need to channel his thoughts or he would go insane, a common fear among veterans who had fought in World War II or Vietnam and who were exposed to some of the most brutal experiences of mankind ever.

To survive he devised a mental visualization program of playing a round of golf at his favorite golf course back home. He visualized every small detail and utilized all his senses to put himself on the course.

He imagined the clothes he would wear, the smell of the freshly cut grass, the wind blowing against his skin, the warmth of the sun, and the sounds of the birds. He imagined the club in his hands, the swing of the club, and the flight of the ball on every single hole on the eighteen-hole golf course.

He did this *every day* for the entire seven years! When he was released and returned home, he was physically a shadow of himself.

He loved to play golf but was quite average at the game and shot in the mid to low nineties prior to his Vietnam assignment. Once home, he decided to play his first round of golf. Hesitant, as he had not swung a club in seven years, he played at his favorite course.

He shot an unimaginable round of seventy-four. He had cut twenty strokes off his average! How? The power of visualizing helped him recall the perfect swing, the nuances of every hole, and the relaxation and joy of playing.

The mind is a powerful tool if our visual behavioral rehearsal is repeatedly practiced.

Powerful Techniques of Visualization

In addition to the training one can receive from this audio file, Top Gun performers can practice additional visualization techniques.

The first is referred to as *visual motor behavioral rehearsal* (vmbr). This technique was first utilized by some of the greatest golfers in the past seventy-five years. At first they just visualized but later learned that there was a psychological technique that best described it. Ben Hogan first used this technique, and later the great Jack Nicklaus perfected it.

vmbr involves visual–motor (muscle)–behavioral–rehearsal. As Nicklaus would stand over a ball, he would visualize his entire shot—by rehearsing his swing visually and feeling his muscles react as he imagined the ball landing gently on the green and then execute the perfect swing each time, before he hit the ball. This process readies and activates the muscle memory and the pathways of the brain to produce the desired outcome.

The VMBR technique is a powerful tool that Top Gun performers can use in competition in sports and work—swinging a golf club, batting a baseball, kicking a field goal, hitting a puck into the net, shooting free throws, or making a presentation, trying a court case, performing complex surgery, engaging in an aerial dogfight, or making a quick maneuver to dodge a surface-to-air missile. This audio file utilizes all the senses and trains one to perform at their peak performance level.

We automatically perform VMBR each time we visualize ourselves performing our daily activities of preparing to meet someone, taking a test, and conducting dozens of daily activities that require our best performance.

Steps to Visual Motor Behavioral Rehearsal

To practice for any type of performance in order to bring about maximum success, follow the steps below.

1. Find a quiet place and close your eyes, calm your mind.
2. Relax your body—particularly all your muscles—so as not to be tight as that impedes performance.
3. Visualize a scene for perfect performance utilizing all your senses— hearing, feeling, smelling, tasting—and see it in your mind's eyes with as much detail as possible.
4. Break the action into a chain and link together each step of the perfect performance.
5. Breathe for a smooth performance to allow a fluidness of motion.
6. Continue to repeat as often as necessary to embed the behavior into your mind so that it is automatically programmed without having to "think too much."

Guided Imagery

Guided imagery (GI) is another, more specific visualization technique that has been effective for many years. It is a mind-body intervention whereby a trained therapist or practitioner helps an individual to generate mental images in person or via video or audio files.

Mental imagery, especially visual and auditory imagery, can alleviate a number of physical and mental conditions (Arntz 2012). We treated thousands of patients via biofeedback to heal their pain, calm their nerves, improve their blood pressure, and enhance overall health. The way they see or perceive their physical and mental condition affects their entire biological system, which impacts their immune system and perception of themselves.

We have employed GI techniques in treating patients who have experienced physical or mental trauma that can impede one's performance. One such patient was a renowned lawyer who had been involved in a horrific car accident. Although she was healed from her injuries, the vividness of her experience produced a fear of driving.

By using both GI in our therapy room along with physical biofeedback, particularly electromyography of muscle tightening each time she went to drive, we slowly progressed from relaxation (audio file 1) and breathing exercises (audio file 2) to positive self-talks (audio file 3) and finally visualization (audio file 4) to overcome her fears.

She had not been able to work, as she needed to drive herself to court. By guiding her to first see herself driving and relaxing, to sitting in the car, to finally and gradually driving the car a little more each day, we were able to overcome her mental block.

GI can be a significant adjunct for Top Gun performers who have experienced such episodes by helping to clear out any blockage visually in order to perform at their highest level.

Slump Busting

Ever been in a slump? Every talented Top Gun performer has or will have a slump. A key question is: How does one minimize the frequency, duration, and intensity of a slump?

I was blessed to have an insightful graduate school professor who was not afraid of challenging his students. About midway through a course on psychotherapy and my asking challenging questions as I was treating "emotionally disturbed adolescents" (the label at the time) in a large public school system, my professor challenged me. "What is the matter with you, Stark? You think you have to be perfect. You know in baseball if you bat .300 you can be an all-star!"

I shot back, "I don't strike out seven out of ten times—not me." Perhaps I was arrogant and inexperienced, but I at least was confident in my skills.

But my professor made a big impression on me. He had the courage and caring as well as insight to challenge me. I will never forget the baseball analogy. Nor his caring mentorship.

I was supposed to serve more than one hundred behaviorally impaired adolescents in a year. I had served more than one hundred in the first three months and was proud of myself until I got to my office and found fifty more referrals waiting for me. This was right after seeing a teacher who was attacked by a student and after an hourlong consultation blamed me for not removing the students. No residential options were available!

Always—always keep in mind that no matter how successful you are, there will be barriers that Top Gun performers need to overcome to be successful over their long careers. The barriers are that you will never have enough (1) staff, (2) money, (3) time, (4) or resources, and that you will have to deal with (5) too many people to take care of and (6) politics.

To overcome these barriers and get out of a slump, it's best to stop digging if you are in a hole and get a ladder to climb out. We can best do that by not trying so hard and by focusing on what we are doing wrong.

For example: "Don't see pink elephants! Don't see pink elephants!" What do you see as I say this? Yes, pink elephants.

What do all athletes and high performers do? They watch film of what they did wrong—over and over to correct their behavior. While it is helpful to know what you are doing wrong, I always recommend focusing on what you are doing right.

I suggest going back and finding video of your best speech, reliving the great calls you made in picking winning stocks when you were in the groove, or visualizing your perfect swing—over and over and over. Lock that swing (or other behavior) into the visual cortex of your brain until that is what you see instead of what not to do. Pair the "perfect" visual behavior with the relaxation, breathing, positive self-talks, and mental preparation before you perform, and you will pop out of that slump faster than you can say, "Oh no, here we go again!"

There are many books written on the numerous steps to break out of a slump—but they often make it more complicated than it needs to be, and this process often backfires.

You hear the expressions "See the ball—be the ball," or "I love the way he sees the field," or "I love the vision she has on the court—what a gift." Almost all great Top Gun performers "see" themselves just before performing—giving that speech, making that perfect dive with all the twists and summersaults, or presenting the closing arguments to the jury after a long trial.

Creating a Vivid Vision

One of the most important mental skills we can impart to a Top Gun performer is to give them a *vision* of how to perform rather than *words* about what to do. Of course, communicating in such a way as to create a vivid picture in an individual's mind provides long-term benefits for repeat performance.

For example, I gave one or two presentations—big or small—each week over the past forty years. That comes to more than one thousand presentations. Early on I focused on *content* (lots of data, slides, and so forth), which, while helpful, was far short of my expectations.

I learned to also focus on the *process* to help my audience see what I see.

When we communicate, people hear our words and then try to create a vision in their mind to lock these words into their memory so that the vision may impact how they behave later. If they fail to create that visual imagery, the presentation will fail.

The typical Top Gun performer will hear hundreds of presentations in their lifetime. Ninety-five percent of these presentations will be totally forgotten—what a waste!

A number of years ago a manufacturing plant I was consulting with brought in a motivational speaker (Zig Ziglar). He was the top motivational speaker in the country at the time and presented to some five hundred people for forty-five minutes.

Curious, I interviewed dozens of the attendees two weeks later to find out what they remembered about the presentation. Their response was, "I don't remember anything he said, but he was funny."

In short, he motivated no one, and the five thousand union employees were angry at the waste of spending $45,000 for a brief "motivational" presentation. The CEO who wanted to make a big splash was soon after fired.

From that day on I vowed to "change behavior" as the main purpose of my presentations. How? By creating a vision and leaving people with a motion picture in their head on how to get better by seeing it first.

Remember hearing the great words "a chicken in every pot," associated with Herbert Hoover's presidential campaign, and "a computer . . . in every home," said by Bill Gates of Microsoft fame? These were powerful images that galvanized action for an entire nation.

Top Gun performers far too often use mushy abstract language with catch-phrases that have empty visual messages. Research indicates that leaders, in their communication to others, use conceptual words three to fifteen times more often than they use image-based words (Carton and Lucas 2018).

Asking others to *imagine* the future and how they perform is far more effective in producing vivid imagery than *telling* others to use images. I often find that in training Top Gun performers, the better they can help me get a visual picture in my mind as to their performance, the quicker and better I can improve the outcome. The same is true for me—I have to leave each individual with what to do and how to do it visually. Then by getting them to see and hear my words and repeat it by saying, writing, and doing it, they remember it best.

People Remember
10 percent of what they READ
20 percent of what they HEAR
30 percent of what they SEE
50 percent of what they SEE and HEAR
70 percent of what they SAY and WRITE
90 percent of what they DO!
    (Edgar Dale)

Application of Visualization

Question: What do a heart-transplant surgeon, a nuclear engineer, an NFL quarterback, a NASCAR driver, and a Top Gun pilot have in common? Answer:

These Top Gun performers are exceptional visualizers. They have the ability to clearly *see*, before they exactly perform, how to execute the perfect behavior for the maximum outcome.

HEART SURGEON

My heart surgeon told me at age fifty-five that unless I have complex surgery, I would die in a slow and painful process. That got my attention! He said I was a candidate for a complex double-valve/triple-bypass surgery during a four-hour procedure.

I said, "I hear you are probably one of the top-ten best surgeons in the Midwest for this complex surgery." He looked straight at me and fired back, "I might be one of the top-ten best heart surgeons in the world in this procedure!" You have to love my heart surgeon's confidence! We scheduled surgery on the spot.

There is a great deal of research on how to "mentally" prepare for surgery for a maximum outcome, and relaxation and visualization are a big part of it.

The day after surgery, the surgeon visited me in the intensive care unit and said, "I never missed a stitch." That was revealing. More than a hundred stitches were needed for very delicate work—surgery that he visualized down to the single stitch and clearly remembered the next day. Twenty-five years later I am a "journal article" for going so long without a revision or replacement surgery—unheard of in this type of procedure!

A surgeon with great hands and even better eyes!

NUCLEAR ENGINEER

I was invited to attend and mentor a class at MIT by the CEO of a large utility company. The attendees were in Boston for an intensive training session on the operation of nuclear power plants. The participants were from nuclear plants all across the country and performed different functions.

In consulting for more than ten years with staff of various nuclear plants, I came to respect their enormous responsibility and complexity. The training involved the most amazing psychological evaluation I have witnessed in my entire career.

The entire class visited a simulator of a nuclear plant and was exposed to an intensive exercise called "Scrambling the Plant." Simulators are an exact replica of the actual nuclear control room—lots of panels with lights and danger signs. They were a complete surprise to all the attendees.

"Scrambling the plant" means that a reactor shutdown was triggered—a really big deal! Loud sirens were going off, lights were flashing, and a red phone was ringing to signal that the Nuclear Regulatory Commission's (NRC) office was calling on the hotline. All plants in the area are instantly connected to the NRC and reported to all the nuclear plants in the country in real plant shutdowns.

The psychological reaction was incredibly revealing and shocking! The chief financial officer of one plant immediately questioned whether this warning was really all that important, but after the chief nuclear officer of the course indicated that the feds were calling and he had better have an answer or he would be in big trouble. When he had been informed that his plant could be shut down for months or even years, costing hundreds of millions of dollars as well as his job loss, his face went red, then white, and he looked as if he might pass out.

Also in attendance, the CEO of a large energy company with nuclear plants quickly and calmly picked up the NRC hotline and answered questions despite a fake cell phone call from his wife that he handled perfectly during the entire process. We quickly knew why he was one of the top leaders in the country in this field.

But the most intriguing person was the nuclear engineer and ex–navy submarine officer. As soon as the loud sirens and flashing lights came on, he stood up, forgot that this was a simulation and immediately went to the large panel of blinking lights and took charge.

His visualization of the problem became apparent as he yelled, "Okay, shut down reactor coolant valve 1," and followed this by barking out six additional commands. He actually went inside the nuclear reactor in his mind and quickly resolved the problem while others panicked, just what you would expect from a Top Gun performer with exceptional visual skills.

NFL QUARTERBACK

I was privileged to work with an exceptional college quarterback on his visualization skills, sharing the visualization audio file to help prepare him for instantaneous decision-making.

After two years of working with all the performance techniques and audio files, this young man was selected as a top-ten pick of the NFL draft. He signed for millions and will easily make $100 million over his career with a possibility of being a Hall of Famer as a top-five quarterback in the NFL.

The primary learning tool in almost all collegiate and pro sports is video and audio file analysis. Hundreds of hours of minute review of plays help the quarterback hone his skills to better "see" the field and "read" the defense or opposition. In a sport or in the business world, split-second decisions require exceptional visual skills to "see the field" or see how to solve a crisis problem.

NASCAR DRIVER

In NASCAR I was asked to work with the top drivers in the world over a sixteen-year period. Such classy individuals as Jeff Gordon, Jimmy Johnson, Dale Earnhardt Jr., and Brian Vickers allowed me to be a part of some eight championships and hundreds of wins.

My training with a total of twenty-three drivers and twenty-six crew chiefs at Hendrick Motorsports in the NASCAR sport produced some special memories and lifelong friendships.

It is stunning to watch a powerful car reach more than two hundred miles per hour into a corner and hope the wheels "stick" and do not hit the wall. The eyesight and visual systems of the drivers are so fine-tuned that they can drive that fast inches apart as their cars almost float due to the wind aerodynamics.

These drivers hone their visual skills via simulators. Almost all of the drivers have simulators in their homes, and every track is recorded with each bump, curve, braking, banking, and acceleration programmed into the computer.

Fractions of seconds add up over a four-hundred-lap race, and those with exceptional visual cues to react instantly emerge as winners in the wake of those who crash and get lapped. Just think about being one-tenth of a second slower than the leader over four hundred laps. That's four hundred times one-tenth of a second, or forty seconds, which means you, the driver, just got lapped and finished last, as it takes forty seconds to travel one lap on a short track.

TOP GUN PILOT

The best of the best. As Top Gun pilot Carter describes, at speeds exceeding the speed of sound, seconds can mean the difference between success and tragedy. Visualization is his most critical skill. Refueling midflight, landing on an aircraft carrier in windy seas with the carrier rising and falling dangerously, and avoiding incoming missiles while engaging in intense dogfights require exceptional visual skills, as described in earlier chapters.

The Future of Visualization

A breakthrough in wireless technology will take our ability to visualize as a mental skill to an entirely new level. The fifth generation of cellular service, or 5G, brings speeds ten to one hundred times faster than today's technology.

The biggest impact will be in virtual and augmented reality. Remote operations using robotics in offsite locations and millions of cheap, low-powered sensors will allow a look inside nuclear reactors. NASCAR drivers and quarterbacks will wear goggles to simulate competition and teach adjustments with total sensory input.

Our learning curve will accelerate, and body sensors will tell us how we are reacting via blood pressure, brain waves, heart rate, and other total body measures.

Conclusion

The use of this visualization training audio file is designed to improve performance by Top Gun performers across settings—work, school, and sports—and across skill sets to build on the other mental skills via the audio files.

The ancient philosophers, particularly Socrates, Plato, and Aristotle, taught us that the main goal in life is to "know thyself" (*gnothi seauton*).

Each of the six mental skills augmented with the audio files and the material in each chapter can produce dramatic results and allow Top Gun performers to maintain their exceptional level of performance over a long period of time.

9

Hypnosis—Peak Performance

Hypnosis is one of the most fascinating yet least
understood concepts in psychology.
—HANS-EYSENCK, BRITISH PSYCHOLOGIST (1916–97)

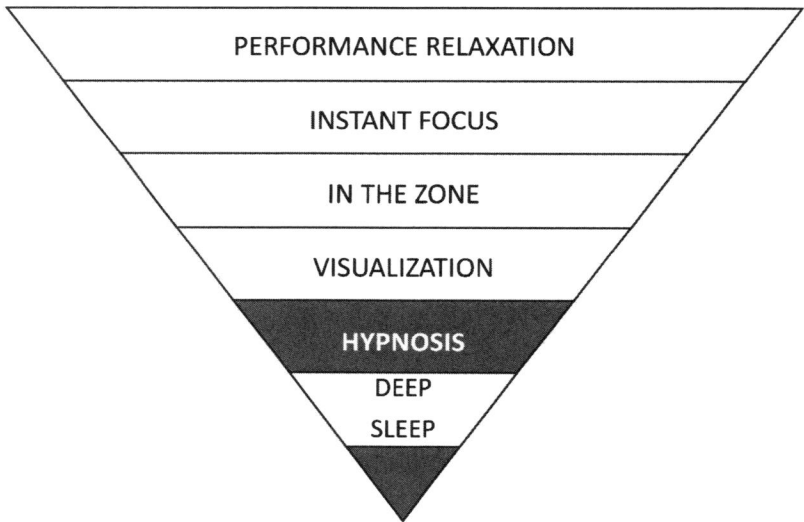

Fig. 24. Performance enhancement skills: Hypnosis. Created by Jack Stark.

It's the biggest game of the year!

It's also the biggest game of our star player's career: senior night, the last home game of the season for a three-time all-American and national player of the year—very special. The setting is a packed arena in Omaha, Nebraska, for Creighton University basketball versus the top Big East team.

One hour before tip-off and the eighteen-thousand-capacity arena already is almost full. There is an electric, vibrating buzz in the crowd. Senior night will be a special and emotional night for four amazing seniors, because it's the last home game of their college careers.

Warren Buffett is on the floor high-fiving the players during early shootarounds. The music volume is pumped up, and the hard rock song "Black Betty"—the African American work song—has the juices flowing.

Our star player Doug McDermott is in a side room with the lights off and lying on a training table. We are about to do our traditional pregame hypnosis and focus session, and I am concerned that he could be too emotional for the night. After all, it's his last home game being coached by his father, head coach Greg McDermott.

Most players in this situation come out *too* hyped and fail to perform to their high standards. But not tonight! Doug has a look about him that I had never seen before in our four years of doing this pregame routine for *every single game*, home and away.

His jaw was locked, eyes forward, and he looked slightly angry. Whoa! I knew tonight would be different.

We do our fifteen-minute session of relaxation, visualization of plays, and building energy and confidence in every cell of his body. He was ready! Polite, thankful, humble, and appreciative as always. The very best athlete I have worked with over my forty-year career. A young man we would all be proud to have as a son.

Yes, I have been blessed to work with more than a hundred players in college sports who went on to have pro careers. From Heisman Trophy winners, offensive and defensive players of the year, and gold medal Olympians to dozens of highly ranked professional draftees with long careers.

Doug McDermott is by far the best athlete, including members of the twenty-two national championship teams I was privileged to have been a part of. The March 17, 2014, cover of *Sports Illustrated* was a full picture of the player of the year in college and the three-time all-American. The headline on the cover read "College Basketball's Secret Weapon—The Hypnotic Doug McDermott." As was typical of this classy young man, the story was about him, but he humbly made it about all the others who helped him.

We were playing a conference rival—the Providence Friars—and they were desperate for a road win. Providence double-teams and triple-teams Doug (a six-foot-eight-inch, 230-pound forward) all night. From the starting whistle, Doug was focused and aggressive, and he played the game of his life.

I kept the stat sheet. Doug, despite the swarming defense, scored forty-five points. He was 17-25 for an astounding 68 percent shooting, five of seven from the three-point line and seven rebounds. We won 88–73, with Doug scoring more than half the points.

Surely the most emotional moment of his life was near the end of the game when he broke the three-thousand-point mark for his four seasons. This rare feat had been accomplished by only five previous players in the history of college basketball. Timeout was called by his father—Coach presented him with the game ball and a huge hug. Both men had tears in their eyes. The crowd went wild with a standing ovation. We all cried.

Doug went on to become the NCAA scoring champion in 2014. He was the consensus national college player of the year as a senior in 2014 and finished with the fifth-most points in NCAA Division I men's basketball history. Doug was awarded thirteen national trophies for his accomplishments and was the eleventh overall pick of the NBA draft to the Chicago Bulls. He played for seven NBA teams over a twelve-year career. We even continued the pregame sessions for four years into his pro career.

What Is Hypnosis?

The American Psychological Association defines hypnosis as a technique in which clinicians make suggestions to individuals who have undergone a procedure designed to relax them and focus their minds. Hypnosis is a state in which a person seems to be asleep but can still see, smell, hear, and respond to things said to them.

The focused attention enhances one's capacity to respond to suggestions for improved performance.

During hypnosis, a person is said to have heightened focus and concentration. It allows for one to concentrate intensely on a specific thought or memory while blocking out sources of distraction.

Hypnosis is comparable to daydreaming. When you dream you tend to block out other thoughts that are present and simply focus on your daydream. It is comparable to quiet relaxation with your eyes closed, meditation, deep prayer, or mindfulness visualization. During a hypnosis session one focuses fully on what is going on in the immediate moment and is not distracted by thoughts and sounds.

Hypnosis has been approved by the American Medical, Dental, and Psychological Associations as long as it is performed by a trained therapist or health-care provider professional (Leslie 2000).

A new definition of hypnosis derived from academic psychology was provided in 2005 when the Society for Psychological Hypnosis, a division of the American Psychological Association, published the formal definition that best describes the entire process.

"Hypnosis typically involves an introduction to the procedure during which the subject is told that suggestions for imaginative experiences will be presented. The hypnotic induction is an extended initial suggestion for using one's imagination and may contain further elaboration of the introduction. A hypnotic procedure is used to encourage and evaluate responses to suggestions. When using hypnosis, one person (the subject) is guided by another (the hypnotist) to respond to suggestions for changes in experience, alterations in perception, sensation, emotion, thought or behavior" (Leslie 2000).

Approvals of hypnosis first came from the British Medical Association in 1892 and the American Medical Association in 1958. Viewed as a safe and valuable wellness modality, hypnosis is taught at many leading medical and dental schools as a treatment approach for both surgical and nonsurgical procedures.

What Hypnosis Is Not

There are many myths about hypnosis. The most prevalent is that the hypnotist has "power" over the person in a trance, which of course is not true. The person being hypnotized is not forced to do anything that is suggested.

Another myth is that one can lose consciousness and be controlled by the process. Unfortunately, many individuals get their perceptions from TV, movies, and fiction novels. They see individuals make animal noises, sing songs, and behave bizarrely. These behaviors are what we in the profession refer to as *stage hypnosis* as opposed to *medical hypnosis*.

It is strictly unethical for a psychologist, physician, or therapist to engage in stage, or entertainment, hypnosis. Ethical standards in professional organizations are explicit that trained professionals can lose their licenses to practice this type of treatment.

In the 1950s and 1960s stage hypnosis was a popular entertainment but was considered to be an extension of magic by a showman. Stage hypnosis, which is a theatrical performance, has little in common with clinical-medical hypnosis—just as a Hollywood movie doesn't reflect real life.

My first time meeting a stage hypnotist was more than thirty years ago at a comedy club. The performer was funny and entertaining, and was different from what I had seen at Vegas shows where individuals from the audience volunteered. The subjects seemed to be under the control of the hypnotherapist and behaved in all kinds of bizarre ways. It did seem to me that a number were staged audience "plants," along with a few who drank too much and wanted to see if hypnosis would work.

The comedy club performer told us that only really smart people could be hypnotized, so immediately I thought, "Well, gee, I'm smart. After all, I have a PhD," and began to feel quite relaxed. Then it dawned on me what was happening.

Afterward I asked the performer about his training, and he told me he had received his PhD in clinical psychology many years earlier from Duke University. Duke is well known for its research in the area of paranormal psychology. He said he took an elective course on hypnosis. He had had a heart attack from too much stress in treating patients, and the doctors recommended something less stressful. He quit his practice and left the field to travel the country and entertain in comedy clubs.

I experienced confusion about and objection to hypnosis from a prominent coach at a top-five football program. He was a receivers coach and was very spiritual. I explained that players do not lose control of their minds and that hypnosis is simply very similar to deep prayer or meditation.

Pregame hypnosis helped receivers to visualize their routes and blocking assignments. A number of the receivers went on to become significant players in the NFL.

In short, stage hypnotists may persuade a subject to make noises or act weird, but no hypnotist can persuade a subject to hurt or kill someone like we see in the movies.

Hypnosis Caution

Top Gun performers are smart and cautious, as they can usually spot "fake" professionals. It is wise to carefully check out the credentials of anyone offering such services.

Stage hypnotists are entertainers; they are not clinicians, nor are they licensed professionals. If professional services in this area are desired, the best prepared are psychologists, psychiatrists, dentists, nurses, clinical social workers, and physicians. This group is highly regulated and licensed to practice.

Special training is also desired by such groups as the American Society of Clinical Hypnosis (ASCH) and the Society for Clinical and Experimental Hypnosis (SCEH).

The extensive and continued training we have received from the ASCH in this area as well as our treatment of a large population of Top Gun performers across a wide span of issues has prepared us well to provide these specialized services for forty years.

History of Hypnosis

The origins of hypnosis are often traced back to the late 1700s, when a German doctor by the name of Franz Anton Mesmer claimed to provide medical and psychiatric cures. His flamboyant and grand demonstrations of what he called "animal magnetism" offended many in the medical and psychological community.

Pushback and investigations by the political medical establishments claimed he was a fraud. The term "mesmerized" stuck and is used extensively as a description of the process in the history of hypnosis.

In the 1800s the British medical community revived the use of hypnosis until the use of anesthesia—ether and other chemicals—was found to be more effective in surgery. Today hypnosis is being more widely used outside surgery for the treatment of numerous physical, mental, and emotional disorders. Hypnosis is not a therapy or a treatment but a technique used as an adjunct to enhance performance by a well-trained professional.

Application

Hypnosis has been successfully used to treat the following psychological and physiological conditions.

Psychological
Pain
Anxiety
Stress
Depression
Fears
Habit disorders
Trauma—mental
Abuse
Performance enhancement
PTSD

Physiological
Irritable bowel syndrome
High blood pressure
Headache
Birth (patients prefer a natural process or are allergic to anesthesia)
Smoking cessation
Weight loss
Pre- and postsurgical recovery

This clinician has successfully used hypnosis in all of these areas as an adjunctive technique to treat individuals with both mental and physical challenges. Along with other techniques such as biofeedback, relaxation, visualization, and cognitive behavior therapy, hypnosis can be a powerful tool with the right person at the right time.

Hypnosis is not for everyone or for every challenge. The only real limitation found in the use of the self-hypnosis audio file is one's motivation to listen to it and the ability to focus on its instructions.

I first started using hypnosis with athletes in the 1970s and with patients in a medical clinic in the 1980s. I was embedded in the internal medicine department of a large medical clinic with hundreds of physicians in both primary care and specialties such as OB/GYN, cardiology, ophthalmology, pediatrics, and orthopedics.

I was the only non-MD in the group but a full partner. It was an amazing practice with a model decades ahead of its time, as today this process of working beside physicians is recommended by all professional groups as the gold standard of care.

I was eager in the 1980s to prove my worth. I suggested to the medical group upon my initial presentation that my goal was to assist them by either reducing the number of medications or eliminating their use altogether. Needless to say, the older physicians were skeptical.

I was quickly booked and was seeing fifty or more patients a week for an hour each. I was forced to find an alternative to the practice of everyone getting a prescription for a pill from their referring physician.

There are only three things that can happen with patients who seek treatment: (1) surgery, (2) medication, and (3) a change in behavior. Changing behavior requires more work and often requires weeks or months of treatment.

The essential element of this process is holding the person responsible for their own behavior. Medication and surgery are something that is given to you in a passive, receiving way. Changing behavior, however, is an active process that gives an individual the confidence they need to improve their performance when, where, and how they want to perform.

Using these audio files sequentially is a fast, cheap, and powerful learning tool that empowers an individual to change. Individuals walked out of our office with an audio file downloaded to their phone and could use them anytime, thereby reducing their dependence on medication either altogether or at a lower dosage.

My first application with an outstanding athletic Top Gun performer occurred in 1996. I had just come off an emotional year in which our university football team (Nebraska) won the national championship with an undefeated season.

The team had been voted the fourth-best sports team of the twentieth century by ESPN: first, the 1927 Yankees; second, the 1977 Montreal Canadiens; third, the 1985 Chicago Bears; and fourth, the 1995 University of Nebraska Huskers.

The basketball team had a good year in 1995, but Nebraska's star player in 1996 was a sophomore, Tyronn Lue, from Missouri. Tyronn was excited, as we were playing our first conference game against top-twenty-ranked Texas.

Tyronn had a terrific game, his best game to date against a really good team that we beat. Excited afterward, he was interviewed by a TV analyst, who asked Tyronn what happened as he went "off" for twenty-three points and won the game for the team. His response, "Man, that Dr. Stark—he took me into the back room and 'hyp-no-tized' me." We all got a laugh out of that one.

Tyronn went on to national honors and was a first-round NBA pick (twenty-third) and played for the Lakers. After an eleven-year NBA playing career, he went into coaching and eventually won the NBA national championship with LeBron James and the Cleveland Cavaliers. A terrific young man, a great leader, and a person admired by everyone, he is now the head coach of the NBA's Los Angeles Clippers and is recognized as a terrific talent.

Guided Self-Hypnosis

Hypnosis can be done in two different ways: either by another person—a professionally trained individual—which is referred to as heterohypnosis, or by self-hypnosis. While both styles can be effective, those who perfect self-hypnosis can enter into just as deep a trance, if they practice the process, as can be achieved with the therapist-guided approach. Obviously, a professional who conducts a hypnosis session can observe and adjust the process to maximize a deeper trance. It is not easy to learn to do self-hypnosis by yourself initially without a lot of practice.

The use of audio file 5 is essentially a "guided" self-hypnosis, during which you hear my voice and are guided through the process with a goal of significantly improving your performance. The audio file is designed to be a short (fourteen-minute) hypnosis session with a mild to moderate level of trance.

Questions you may ask are "Does it work?" and "Does it work across ages, gender, school, sports, work, and live situations requiring a focused 'peak performance'?" The answer to both questions is "Yes!" People aged five to ninety-five with different levels of understanding may undergo hypnosis designed for general use in all situations requiring a focused, relaxed, and extraordinary performance.

Having utilized this audio file with thousands of Top Gun performers, I never cease to be amazed at its effectiveness, especially when one considers its simplicity, cost, ease of use, and lack of side effects.

Using the audio file is in a sense a guided process by me taking you through the steps, as opposed to doing it on your own. After extensive use, however, it becomes an easy project to use the format to audio file your own voice.

Hypnosis Process

Many people will tell you they can't be hypnotized—perhaps due to motivation. But I have rarely encountered someone who can't have some level of hypnotic trance, whether in person or using the audio file.

Some individuals are able to immediately enter into a deeper trance, while others who have difficulty in "quieting the mind" take more time but eventually attain at least a mild to moderate level of hypnosis. Research indicates that only about 10 percent of the population can be categorized as being "highly hypnotizable," while others are less likely to enter into a deep state of hypnosis. Perhaps the reason that people who undergo stage hypnosis can quickly achieve a deeper trance is that practitioners of stage hypnosis "cull" individuals from a large audience down to a few who are highly motivated to participate.

The same is true for individuals who claim one session of hypnosis helped them quit smoking, lose weight, or eliminate an addictive habit. It happens but only rarely. If only it was that simple. Placebo can be powerful.

Sessions often need to be repeated many times to gain the desired outcome.

When I have applied the hypnosis process to groups, it is still effective but less so, as a few in the large group cough, fidget, and otherwise prevent the others from initially entering into a deep trance. Most eventually benefit, however, if adjustments are made to assure a deeper trance.

Our experience is that those using the audio file 5 sometimes go into a deeper trance and almost don't want to come out of it, as it's the calmest and most relaxed they have been in a long time. It's as if they want or need to sleep or deeply relax from all of the stress in their life.

Hypnosis Stages

STAGE 1: RELAXATION

This is the stage where the Top Gun performer finds a quiet, dark, and comfortable place to relax and begin the process. Noise can cause distractions, bright light keeps one too alert, and a comfortable bed or couch facilitates a quicker and deeper level of relaxation.

STAGE 2: THE TRANCE

The audio file will gradually take a person through a series of steps or levels from alert to deeply relaxed whereby one shuts down all distractions, worries, and expectations.

STAGE 3: EMBEDDED SUGGESTIONS

In this stage suggestions are offered to be adopted to improve confidence, performance, and visualized outcomes to achieve one's desired goals.

STAGE 4: BEHAVIORAL OUTCOMES

In this final stage one is gradually brought back from a deep state of relaxation to wakefulness with encouragement to perform those behaviors implanted in one's subconscious over the next few hours and days.

Hypnosis and the Brain

Researchers at Stanford University School of Medicine found the specific sections of the brain that alter activity and connections during a hypnotic state. Researchers found decreases in activity in the dorsal anterior cingulate cortex, an area of the brain that is the "quieting network."

There are reduced connections between two major parts of the brain (prefrontal cortex and cingulate cortex). The reduced connectivity between these areas allows a person to engage in suggestion during hypnosis.

Hypnosis and Performance Research

Hypnotic visualization can help one overcome performance anxiety in the achievement of personal goals (Pearce 1997). It pushes participants to see their ideal selves and directs their minds in a positive direction (Garver 1990).

In a declarative memory task, subjects under hypnosis had better recall than a control group had, suggesting that hypnosis can lead to better memory consolidation (Schichl et al. 2011).

Research has indicated that the more clearly one is able to experience mental images and control imagined movements, the more likely one can translate these images into improved performance. Just imagining yourself performing a sports skill causes EMG activity in the musculature resembling that which would occur during the actual physical execution of the skill. The EMG pattern is not completely identical, but the neural impulses passed from the brain to the muscular system during the imagery can be retained in memory as if the movement had actually happened (Schmidt et al. 2017).

Anxiety was significantly decreased in a group of athletes after a hypnosis session compared with a control group (Krenz, Gordin, and Edwards 1985). Hypnosis studies have shown that hypnotic training may increase personal control overflow and athletic performance (Pates, Oliver, and Maynard 2001; Cohn 1991; Pates and Maynard 2000).

A study of hypnosis and basketball performance evaluated the effectiveness of hypnotic suggestions on increased concentration and the ability to make the basket appear larger than its normal size to improve shooting performance. Participants in the hypnosis condition had higher cumulative scores four weeks into the basketball season than the control group had (Schreiber 1991).

In another study, golf athletes listened to daily prerecorded audio files of hypnotic scripts. All participants reported an increase in flow and performance, relaxation, confidence, and focus (Pates, Oliver, and Maynard 2001).

Hypnosis seems to have a positive effect on flow states. This finding has far-reaching implications for athletes because flow states are strongly associated with athletes' best performances (Cohn 1991).

Self-hypnosis can help an athlete sharpen focus, develop mental and physical strength, and increase skill. Hypnosis brings a participant into a heightened state of awareness and concentration, uninhibited by distraction. "When the subconscious is shown repeated images of how the desired result looks and feels, it can go about making the body carry out all of the necessary actions to make these images real" (O'Brian 2011).

There is some evidence that athletes may be more responsive to hypnosis than nonathletes (Dunlap 2005). Hypnosis can change reality perception by transforming verbal messages into inner images or auditory sensations (activation of occipital and temporal areas) (Del Casale et al. 2012). Hypnosis positively controlled emotions, thoughts, feelings, and perceptions in one subject (Pates 2013).

When to Use Hypnosis

Hypnosis, found on audio file 5, can be used any time a relaxed, focused, and optimal behavioral outcome is desired.

For Top Gun performers in athletics, I recommend the audio file an hour to a half hour before competition. This timing allows the athlete to begin to shut off all distractions and lock in on the performance needed to be at their best. It helps the athlete shut down negative self-talks, visualize ideal performance, and reduce heart rate, blood pressure, and anxiety.

When you first come out of the trance you will feel extremely relaxed, so much so that it will take about ten minutes before your pre-event or pregame excitement returns. It's like pulling the plug to your TV set and allows one to reset and better prepare for the task at hand.

A perfect example took place with a young UFC fighter with whom I conducted his first prefight hypnosis. An ex-marine and decorated collegiate wrestler was fighting in his first UFC bout and was a heavy underdog against a Brazilian jujitsu seasoned fighter ranked third in the world.

After conducting our session in the fighter's locker room one hour before the fight, I was eager to see how well he would perform.

In the first round he knocked the Brazilian fighter down *four* times with powerful punches and took him down *three* more times with quick moves. Another UFC fighter sitting with me in the crowd yelled to me, "What did you do to him?" after the first-round bell. Unfortunately, he tired, and the more experienced fighter tied him up with a hold to barely win the bout.

The ex-marine, however, received a bonus as the outstanding fighter of the night, as everyone knew he won the fight but lost on points.

The second example occurred with one of the pit-crew members on Jeff Gordon's number 24 NASCAR team.

It was the first time I used hypnosis with the tire changer, and on their first pit stop he was awesome—an 11.6-second pit stop kept Gordon in first place.

On the next stop I saw the pit crew member standing on the pit-wall ledge, waiting for Gordon to pit. I saw how "tight" he was, as his thinking was to do an even better pit stop while waiting for Gordon to come in.

I instantly knew it was going to be a disaster and just walked away. It was a disaster. His 11.6-second first stop turned into an 18-second stop as lug nuts were dropped, and Gordon went from first to twenty-fourth place on a short track and never fully recovered. The next week this individual was let go, unfortunately. We often used the mantra "Go slow to go fast."

Sometimes when we hurry, we tighten up, and this spells disaster for any sport or situation requiring a smooth, fluid performance.

For Top Gun performers in non-sports-related performances such as giving a presentation, addressing your board of directors, leading a conference call on guidance, or conducting a particularly dangerous mission into enemy territory, the goal is the same—maximize your performance with mental clarity and without all the noise and sometimes doubts that can pop into an excited mind.

A perfect example were the disastrous interviews and guidance conference calls by Elon Musk in 2018. This brilliant mind and guiding genius behind Tesla saw a 30 percent drop in the company's stock price because of his flippant behavior on a few occasions and cost the company billions. He recovered but learned to visualize and prepare better for such engagements.

Hypnosis and Trauma

I have been blessed to be invited to give more than one thousand presentations during my career to schools, nonprofits, athletic organizations, Fortune 500 companies, and military leaders. We have learned so much!

When I give talks at churches, I often use an old backpack as part of a demonstration. Everyone can relate to a backpack, even the little kids in attendance, due to their popularity. Being older, however, I bring out an almost-antique backpack for demonstration.

I hold up the backpack and explain that we all have one on our backs all the time—it's just invisible. We are born with one, and it represents all our memories and experiences—both good and bad. I have some books that have had a profound impact on my life such as Victor E. Frankl's *Man's Search for Meaning*. The book recounts his experience as a Jewish psychiatrist placed in Dachau. He recounts how he saw so many people give up and die, but he made a vow to live despite losing family and friends and experiencing the worst conditions and treatment in the history of mankind. His book is about his will to live. He later used this experience to treat patients in his psychiatry practice.

In the book, Frankl quotes Friedrich Nietzsche: "Those who have a 'why' to live, can bear with almost any 'how.'"

Then I hold up a large rock to represent some childhood memories. Not big, bad memories but the kind that toughens one who lived in a crowded housing project as a youth.

I continue with additional objects to demonstrate that we all carry objects from our past, and we need to let go; otherwise the weight we carry invisibly will weigh us down for life.

In my clinical practice I have seen enough pain and suffering, trauma, and abuse to last four lifetimes. I have found that a type of hypnosis can be very effective in relieving this trauma; it is called age regression hypnosis.

I only mention it here for those who have experienced such childhood or past trauma to consider it as a way to remove a major psychic burden.

Caution should be used, as few people are trained in this area and there have been reported instances of creating false memories by "implanting" memories that did not exist. An experienced therapist, perhaps one trained by the American Society of Clinical Hypnosis, is best suited for the treatment.

I have successfully used this approach with a variety of clients and have been amazed at its effectiveness, but I am highly selective and rarely use this powerful technique. It is exhausting to both the therapist and the client.

Age regression hypnosis invokes taking the subject back in time to an early age to help them recall traumatic experiences and remove them from their backpack and memory as well as possible. This "letting go" allows individuals to move forward in their lives and in some cases forgive those who inflicted trauma.

Three different cases of Top Gun performers come to mind.

The first was a world-class international leader and prominent person in their field. As I took him back to his early years from age four and progressing each year after, I had him raise his finger each time he experienced a traumatic memory in which he was emotionally or physically hurt. I was shocked how frequently he raised his finger. Yet he was able to overcome these experiences and become incredibly successful. Inside, however, there was this unhappiness and perhaps a desire to drive himself to somehow make up for all these painful psychic experiences and memories.

The same thing happened with an international superstar athlete who experienced childhood trauma, and with a high first-round-draft NFL player. Both raised their fingers many times as we progressed through their respective ages.

In all three situations we removed much of the hurt, although it took months and a few years to really see the benefits. In each case the unhappy situation they were in dramatically improved, and they saw a significant increase, on average, in their finances and, even more importantly, a greater sense of happiness and "lightening up" of the backpacks of life.

This procedure is mentioned here, as we have met more individuals who carry a larger burden in life than we ever would have realized. So many carry their silent burdens. If this kind of trauma impacts you, carefully consider such an approach but only with highly trained and experienced individuals.

Conclusion

The use of audio file 5 is carefully chosen as a powerful tool to build on the previous audio files about relaxation, breathing, self-talks, and visualization to incorporate all of them into the hypnotic experience and thus help prepare Top Gun performers for the demanding challenges required of their positions.

10

Deep Sleep

Fatigue makes cowards of us all.
—VINCE LOMBARDI

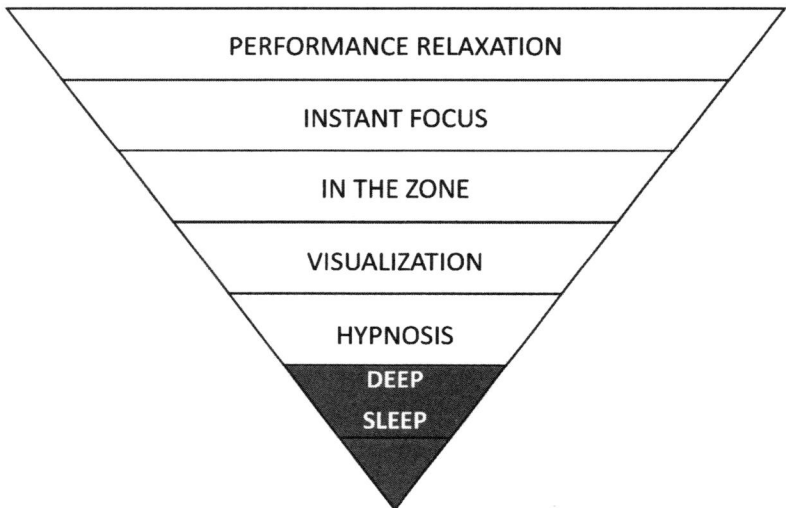

Fig. 25. Performance enhancement skills: Deep sleep. Created by Jack Stark.

What is the number one performance barrier for Top Gun performers? Fatigue!
Lack of energy! It can be traced predominantly to sleep problems.

Description of Sleep

We spend approximately one-quarter to one-third of our lives sleeping. Yet
our knowledge of what actually happens during sleep compared to the rest of
our day is much less understood.

Sleep is a naturally recurring process of our body and mind resting each day during which our consciousness becomes altered. Control of our voluntary muscles, sensory activity, and awareness of our surroundings are all altered. Sleep was originally associated with the Greek word *hypnos*, representing the Greek god of rest.

The American Sleep Association (ASA) is recognized as the top scientific body conducting research and gathering data on this phenomenon, and it serves as our major source of research on sleep.

Sleep patterns vary from one person to another depending on gender, age, work schedule, health, and stress levels. A 2013 Gallup poll of 138 countries indicates that one-third of their citizens experience stress daily and that 51 percent of women and 32 percent of men experience sleep problems due to stress.

We used to think of sleep as a passive process where our body is dormant, but research and medical specialists reveal a very active and dynamic process. Neurotransmitters, or nerve-signaling chemicals, control our sleep by switching on and off our awake and sleep states.

Why Sleep?

In 350 BC Aristotle wrote his essay "On Sleep and Sleeplessness," but there is still much we don't know about why we sleep.

The prestigious magazine *Science* published its 125th anniversary issue in July 2005 and made a list of 125 big questions that remain unanswered by scientists. One of those questions was "Why do we sleep? A sound slumber may refresh muscles and organs or keep animals safe from dangers lurking in the dark. But the real secret of sleep probably resides in the brain, which is anything but still while we're snoring away."

While elusive today, the leading idea is memory consolidation, which involves moving information efficiently around the brain by maintaining the brain circuitry (Kavanu 1997).

Stages of Sleep

Sleep has five stages. We pass through stages 1, 2, 3, 4, and REM (rapid eye movement) sleep. Each stage is cycled through, and then the process starts again. A complete cycle takes an average of 90 to 110 minutes, with each stage lasting 5 to 15 minutes. We cycle through all stages of non-REM and REM sleep four or five times during a typical night with increasingly longer, deeper REM periods occurring toward morning. Fifty percent of our sleep time is in stage 2, 20 percent is in REM, and 30 percent is in stages 1, 3, and 4.

Stage 1: Light sleep—drifting in and out of sleep; muscle activity slows; easily awakened.

Stage 2: Brain waves slow, and eye movements stop. Body begins to prepare for deep sleep; heart rate slows and temperature drops.

Stage 3: Extremely slow brain waves (delta waves) begin to appear. This is a deep sleep, and in this stage people can experience sleepwalking and night terrors.

Stage 4: Brain waves are all delta waves. It is difficult to wake someone in this deep sleep. If awakened, one feels groggy and disoriented.

REM Stage: Breathing is rapid, shallow, and irregular; eyes jerk rapidly and muscles freeze; heart rate increases. This is our dream state and occurs about seventy to ninety minutes after we fall asleep. Some researchers speculate that the brain may "shiver" during REM and provides us the deepest sleep, in order to process and categorize our stored short- and long-term memories.

Extent of Sleep Disorders

The ASA estimates that 80 million U.S. adults have chronic, long-term sleep disorders and an additional 20 million experience occasional sleeping problems. This is close to half the adult population, but sleep issues are of particular interest for Top Gun performers who require and expend a great deal of energy each day.

We spend $80 billion in medical costs and medications each year on sleep disorders alone, while lost productivity costs are an estimated $400 billion—twice that of the United Kingdom, Germany, and Japan combined. More than seventy sleep disorders have been identified. Most common are insomnia, sleep apnea, and restless leg syndrome.

Insomnia tends to increase with age and affects 40 percent of women and 30 percent of men—with 5 percent of adults on long-term sleeping pills.

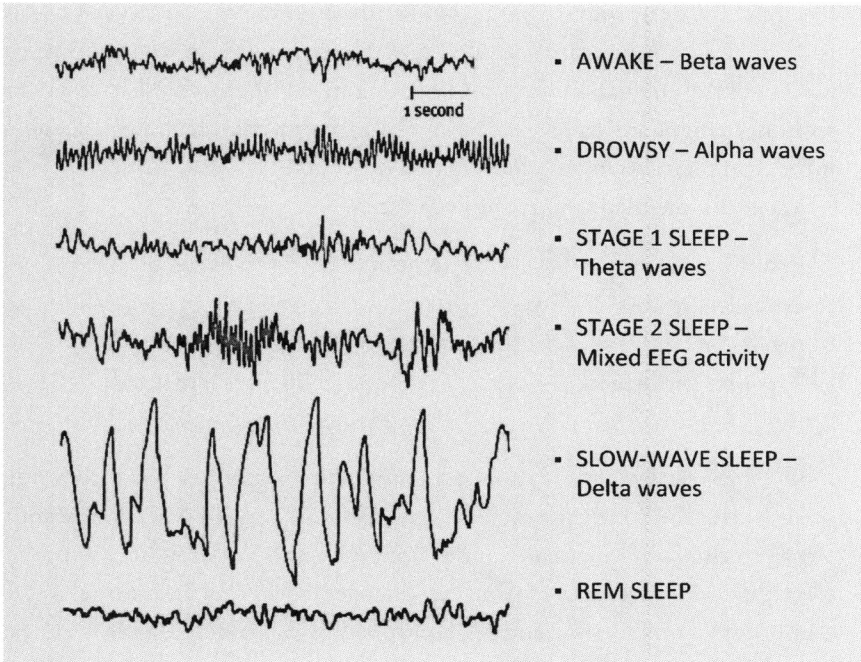

Fig. 26. Stages of brain waves during sleep. Created by Jack Stark.

The National Highway Traffic Safety Administration estimates that one hundred thousand motor vehicle accidents and two thousand deaths are caused by driver fatigue each year. An American Automobile Association study of in-vehicle camera footage showed that drowsiness was a key factor in 9.5 percent of all crashes.

On a personal note, I will never forget the phone call I received at 2 a.m. from an all-American player who was extremely upset that he had fallen asleep while driving home to campus after a weekend break. He had not been drinking, but his car crossed the line briefly, an oncoming car swerved off the road, and a four-year-old boy who was not buckled in was killed. One never forgets.

Amount of Sleep

The National Sleep Foundation via their survey research found the average adult sleeps six hours and fifty-one minutes on workdays but needs a minimum of seven hours; the foundation recommends seven to nine hours each night. A century ago, Americans averaged nine hours a night. In Japan about 40 percent of the population sleeps six hours per night. Those who sleep less than six hours a night are 40 percent more likely to get a cold than those sleeping more than seven hours a night.

The recommended amount of sleep varies.

Infants	16 hours a day
Teenagers	9 hours
Adults	7–8 hours
Top Gun performers	8–9 hours solid, uninterrupted sleep each day

If you are sleep-deprived, it is best to catch up by going to bed early while getting up at the same time each day to allow your body to synchronize your circadian rhythm ("circadian" comes from the Latin for "around or approximately a day"). Circadian rhythms are changes in physical and mental states that occur during the day and are controlled by our biological clock in the hypothalamus area of the brain.

Impact of Sleep Deprivation on Performance

A review of the best research studies revealed the following:

Sleep deprivation increases fatigue, irritability, concentration difficulties, disorientation, and changes in mood (Bonnet 2005).

Sleep is vital for the brain's ability to adapt to input, removal of waste products from brain cells, immune function, and metabolism.

Individuals who self-reported naturally occurring sleep problems showed higher scores of anxiety, depression, and somatic complaints (Tkachenko et al. 2014).

When someone is sleeping, the endocrine system increases the secretion of growth hormone from the pituitary gland, which promotes physiological restitution (Akerstedt and Nilsson 2003).

Getting less than six hours of sleep per night for four or more consecutive nights has been shown to impair immune function, cognitive performance, mood, glucose metabolism, and appetite regulation (Halson 2014).

Top Gun performers who report poor quantity and quality of sleep were rated significantly lower on interpersonal effectiveness (Nowack 2017).

Impact on Athletic Performance

Sleep deprivation can compromise athletic performance by increasing distractibility (Anderson and Horne 2006). It also can impair cognitive performance by reducing visual processing capacity (Kong, Soon, and Chee 2011).

After one night of sleep deprivation among participants in one study, energy, concentration, and speed of thought all declined significantly, in comparison with levels after a night of regular sleep (Klumpers et al. 2015).

Reduction in both quantity and quality of sleep could result in autonomic nervous system imbalance, bringing about symptoms of overtraining syndrome. Sleep loss also could increase proinflammatory cytokines and promote immune system dysfunction (Fullagar et al. 2015). One study showed that just one night of restricted sleep showed decrements in psychomotor functions (Reilly and Deykin 1983).

Obtaining an optimal brain-memory consolidation is important for athletes before and after competition (Stickgold 2005; Mahoney and Avener 1977).

Precompetition anxiety can interfere with and worsen sleep and sleep quality, efficiency, and duration and has been found to dramatically decrease competition performance, according to a study by Juliff, Halson, and Peiffer (2014). The same study showed that out of 283 elite Australian athletes, 64 percent reported poor sleep prior to competition.

A study on performance of college basketball players at Stanford showed that sleep extension during a period of five to seven weeks showed improved shooting accuracy, faster sprint times, faster reaction times, and improved physical recovery (Mah et al. 2011).

Developing and following a regular bedtime and wake time routine is a fundamental sleep hygiene strategy. It promotes optimal sleep and consolidation due to alignment of the circadian timekeeping system. Top Gun performers should avoid sleeping too late in the mornings of off-days, and naps should be carefully chosen. Brief naps of five to thirty minutes improve performance (Stepanski and Wyatt 2003). Naps longer than thirty minutes can throw off your night's sleep by decreasing the body's sleep drive.

An interesting study on night-shift nurses showed that wearing glasses fitted with short-wavelength filters (blue blockers) increased sleep time by forty minutes, reduced wake after sleep onset by around twenty-two minutes, and increased sleep efficiency. Salivary melatonin levels were significantly higher during the following night compared with a control group. This study shows that wearing short-wavelength filtered glasses after a competition or late-night practice could be a good sleep hygiene strategy (Rahman et al. 2013).

Sleep Improvement Tips

It's best to not sleep in beyond one hour on weekends unless you have sleep deprivation of less than five hours each day during the week on average. If you are sleep-deprived, then it's important to restore your insulin levels and lower your risk of diabetes. Just don't make a habit of it.

Taking a short power nap of half an hour can enhance performance, alertness, and attention, particularly if you do it early in the afternoon, that is, before 3 p.m., and not too close to bedtime. Many athletes are huge believers in pregame naps for boosting performance. Cuddling with a significant other releases oxytocin, a secreted hormone that decreases anxiety and promotes relaxation.

Exposure to sunlight is important. If you can get sunshine for just ten minutes shortly after you wake up, it will help shut off melatonin production and increase alertness.

"Never stay up late for something you wouldn't get up early for," says Dr. C. Winter, owner of Charlottesville Neurology and Sleep Medicine. If you are waking up in the middle of the night, play the relaxation (no. 1) and deep sleep (no. 6) audio files. To facilitate falling asleep, quiet the mind, read, shut off all electronics, particularly blue screen light from laptops and iPads.

Sleep Guidelines

Sleep deprivation can cause anxiety, heart problems (atrial fibrillation and atrial flutter), weight gain, memory loss, moodiness, loss of focus, low energy, and decreased performance. Much has been written about the United States being a sleep-deprived nation. The pace of today's society and its stress levels require careful attention to the tremendous benefits of a healthy sleep routine.

Top Gun performers expend and need exceptional amounts of energy to meet the demands of performing at the top 5 percent level in corporate settings, high-speed maneuvers in F-4 Phantom jets, and the grind of professional or college athletics. Individualized sleep routines are necessary to regulate bodily functions and restore health, growth, memory, and happiness. Consider a sleep chart that records when you go to bed and get up and the quality of your sleep, along with any sleep distractors.

Listed below are six guidelines for Top Gun performers to follow for such high levels of performance.

Cold. Think of cavemen and cavewomen. Caves were cold, dark, and wet. The first component necessary for a healthy night of sleep is to maintain a cool bedroom or sleeping area. When the body is warm, it produces less melatonin, a hormone secreted by the brain that helps us enter the sleep cycle. Keep your bedroom temperature between 65 and 75 degrees at night, the optimal being 65 to 72 degrees. Gradually reduce the temperature until you find the right setting. There is some evidence that wearing socks can improve quality of sleep.

Dark. Keep your bedroom as dark as possible. Light stimulates alertness and decreases the release of melatonin. That is why TVs, computers, iPads, and cell phones (especially devices that emit blue light) prevent sleep. Top Gun performers who often engage in international travel or time-zone changes need to take steps (mask, curtains, etc.) to block out bright light just as they are entering deep midmorning sleep often during air travel. Daylight is particularly challenging for night shift workers and others who sleep during the day and require light control measures.

Wet. Keep your room moist. A simple, cheap gauge can monitor the humidity in your bedroom. We recommend quality humidifiers for home and small portable ones on the road. Parts of the country can be particularly dry and thus interrupt fluid breathing because of dry mouth, nose, and throat. We recommend also using saline solution (natural salt water) purchased at drugstores for daytime use and particularly on airplanes when dry air causes colds and sinus infections to flourish. When staying in hotels, turn the temperature down to allow you to fall asleep easily and turn off any fan, as it dries the air.

You can also fill the sink or tub with water and increase room humidity by running the shower briefly.

Eighteen million American adults have sleep apnea. Sleep apnea is a condition, caused by aging, facial structure, and weight, in which the throat and tongue muscles relax and block the airway during sleep. While more prevalent in men, it also impacts women as they approach menopause. Those who are overweight or have large athletic bodies are also prone to sleep apnea. But even those with a smaller frame can require a sleep aid to prevent this dangerous lack of oxygen to the brain and body. If you experience significant snoring or gaps in your breathing patterns at night, it is strongly recommended that you get tested for obstructive sleep apnea. Traditional testing involved monitoring your sleep pattern in a sleep lab all night by a pulmonologist reading your findings. It was often expensive and not always paid for by insurance; also, sleep could be difficult in a foreign bed with electrodes attached to your head. Home recording versions of the test involving wearing a beltlike device around your chest. The technology is better now, and testing is often handled by a primary care physician. Portable compact CPAP machines, which provide continuous positive airway pressure, are available for travel. CPAP machines are used extensively for heart and lung disorders, but elite athletes often require this device too. We have frequently traveled with pro teams and see big linemen or tall basketball players carry their small portable CPAP machines on and off airplanes.

Presleep hygiene. Find a comfortable pillow, mattress, and bedroom along with the cold-dark-wet conditions conducive to relaxed sleep.

Cognitive-behavior techniques. Top Gun performers are often perfectionistic, pay attention to detail, and can become obsessive as discussed earlier. Shutting your brain off particularly at this time of day is hard but necessary. Obsessive rumination keeps the body and mind "revved up" and can either keep one from falling asleep quickly or cause one to wake up early due to worry about unsolved conflicts and other issues. Using audio file 3 techniques here is especially helpful. Cognitive-behavior therapy is as effective as sleeping pills in the short term and more effective in the long term. That's because it treats the cause of insomnia not the symptom, as medication does. The American Academy of Sleep Medicine and the American College of Physicians recommend cognitive behavioral therapy techniques be used first instead of prescribed medications or over-the-counter remedies.

Routine schedules. Going to bed and getting up at the same time during the week is the optimal sleep pattern. Getting eight to ten hours is not always possible. It's best to go to bed an hour or two earlier if you need to catch up on lost sleep. Findings published in the *Journal of Sleep Research* show that sleeping in on weekends is bad for your health and performance. The exception is if you got very little sleep during the week; then you could somewhat catch up. The truth is you can't entirely make up for sleep lost. Reaction time will still be affected by too much weekend sleep, because it can throw off your sleep-wake schedule, making it hard to fall asleep Sunday night, which can mess up performance for the next two or three days. A pattern of sleeping more than two extra hours on weekends increases triglyceride (blood fat) levels, weight gain, diabetes scores, and moodiness. Sleep disturbance is a common challenge among students who are about to take tests or among elite athletes who may play a game on Saturday, stay up late because it's hard to shut down the mind and body, and sleep in on Sunday. Then they are sluggish for the next two days of practice. A classic example is a top college basketball team we worked with that played in a tournament in Vegas. The games ended late, and letting the team have a later curfew on Tuesday night and leave early on Wednesday morning resulted in losses on the following Saturday night in consecutive years. Sleep disruption is also particularly challenging to NBA players playing on consecutive nights or even two days later, as they can finish a game at 10 p.m., fly to another city, get to bed at 3 a.m., and play later that day. More teams are holding out older star players to prevent injury, as the body needs to recover from high-intensity performance. The research is clear also about time-zone changes and performance. There is a high correlation, as East Coast and West Coast teams who travel through two to four time zones can look tired and out of sync due to disruption of their sleep cycles. Also, televised games requiring early-morning or late-night performance offer challenges. Altering practice time to prepare is difficult due to scheduled games, classes, and logistics, and can backfire. Sticking to routine and keeping on their time-zone schedule is best most of the time. Never pull all-nighters, as recovery can take weeks. One team we were working with was a top-five college team that beat a top-ten school the previous week, then traveled to a team that had been a twenty-six-point underdog but beat us. My survey of the starters indicated that a number of them who were engineering majors and seniors pulled all-nighters on their midterms. A few years later I spoke to our national championship team that year and shared that the eighth and ninth weeks of the season we often played poorly even when we won, because all-nighters and resulting sleep disruption were frequent. This week coincided with midterms. I always remind Top Gun performers to get their sleep early in the week and particularly forty-eight hours before a big competition.

Sleep Disruptors

Sleep and wakefulness are impacted by neurotransmitter signals to the brain that in turn are impacted by what we drink, eat, inhale, and medicate ourselves with.

Caffeine. A stimulant in coffee, soft drinks, energy drinks, decongestants, and drugs such as diet pills. Limit intake after 6 p.m. each night. Remember that caffeine is the most widely abused drug in the world.

Antidepressants. Can suppress REM sleep. Weigh the benefits of an antidepressant and other medications on your quality of sleep.

Smoking. Heavy smoking causes light sleep and suppresses REM, and may wake you often after three to four hours of sleep.

Alcohol. Alcohol helps people to fall into light sleep, but deeper stages and REM sleep are often compromised. One should stop drinking one hour before bedtime for every drink consumed, and it is best to avoid alcohol altogether. Researchers are not in agreement on the benefits of even one drink a day. It appears that previous research on the benefits were tainted, as funding for such research came from the alcohol industry. Research presenters at grand rounds in the department of psychiatry at the University of Nebraska Medical School where we worked indicated that the social aspects of drinking, the use of alcohol to briefly reduce anxiety, and an increase in tryptophan from the sugar content of alcoholic drinks helped briefly with depression. Early morning sleep disruption, however, far exceeded any benefit, and perhaps one wakes up craving not so much the alcohol but the feeling of relaxation. For 15 percent of the population who binge drink four times a month, the body never fully recovers from this yo-yo effect. It also makes no sense to eat, sleep, exercise, and do all the right things only to sabotage your own performance by drinking.

Stress. Obsessive thinking and worrying stimulate the body, prevent the release of melatonin, and hinder stages of deeper sleep.

Stimulation. The use of electronic devices, TV, laptops, iPads, and blue-light-emitting devices as well as stimulating activities (e.g., watching *Sports Center* or reruns of games) prevent one from falling asleep immediately.

Sleep Enhancers

After all sleep disrupters are eliminated, significant steps can be taken to enhance sleep and quiet the prefrontal cortex. This part of the brain is associated with recurrent emotions, planning, pain, worry, and unresolved issues, all of which significantly impact performance.

Listed below are the six steps, from least intrusive to most intrusive, that a Top Gun performer can utilize to maximize sleep efficiency. Each step is designed to have the best outcome with the fewest side effects. Top Gun performers can proceed with each step until they reach the level that works best for them.

STEP 1: DEEP SLEEP AUDIO

Like all five previous audio tracks, "Deep Sleep" is designed and recorded by us using extensive research and applied experience with thousands of Top Gun performers, from world leaders and CEOs to elite professional and collegiate athletes.

This audio recording has a hypnotic cadence that facilitates rapid induction of sleep by quieting the mind and shutting off all distractions. Lasting less than ten minutes, it is best used by playing in bed and turning it off as you fall asleep. Or if you wake up in the middle of the night and need to fall back asleep quickly, you can play this audio file then also.

"Deep Sleep" utilizes parts of each of the previous five audio tracks: (1) calmness and relaxation, (2) deep breathing, (3) turning off obsessive thoughts, (4) visualization, and (5) hypnosis. This audio track is the least intrusive and, unlike sleeping pills and over-the-counter remedies, has no side effects on waking. It is fast, cheap, convenient, and practical.

We first utilized this audio file twenty-five years ago with two all-American football players. They were big linemen—six-feet-five or taller and weighing three hundred pounds. When it was explained that this technique would help them with sleep, particularly the night before a game, they were interested but highly skeptical. They were instructed to lie on the training tables and, with the lights turned off, listen to my instructions.

After letting them sleep for half an hour, I noticed pools of saliva had leaked from their mouths, as they were both face down and snoring. It worked! Credibility established.

Players always seemed to have difficulty falling asleep on road trips. So one night I again had two big linemen, so big their feet hung over their beds, and I was in their room sitting on the floor, lights off, putting them to sleep when head coach Tom Osborne, a PhD psychologist himself, opened the door to their room doing bed checks. He saw me and said, "Jack, what are you doing?" Then he said, "Never mind," and quickly shut the door. The players fell into a deep sleep, and I left the room. The next day I talked to them, and they both said they had the best night's sleep in months but got in trouble for oversleeping and missing breakfast!

We have utilized this personal one-on-one approach with competitors ranging from UFC fighters to athletes in the 2016 Rio Olympics.

STEP 2: SLEEPY FOODS

Certain foods help to promote deeper sleep due to their chemical properties. One myth, however, is that drinking a warm glass of milk will help one fall asleep. Milk contains tryptophan, an amino acid that can be conducive to sleep. The problem is you would have to drink two gallons to have any beneficial effect from the tryptophan. Turkey is better—but you can't eat an entire turkey.

A moderate amount of carbohydrate-rich foods seems to increase tryptophan, which is perhaps one reason why we crave these high-calorie comfort foods. Tryptophan increases serotonin and helps us when we are feeling down, but a potential downside is gaining weight.

Avoid high-fat foods, spicy foods, and sugary snacks. Foods that are high on the glycemic index—meaning that the body digests them slowly, only gradually releasing insulin into the bloodstream—are best.

Teas, particularly valerian, have been shown to speed the onset of sleep. The Mayo Clinic's Brent A. Bauer, MD, reports, "Results from multiple studies indicate that valerian—a tall, flowering grassland plant—may reduce the amount of time it takes to fall asleep and help you sleep better. Of the many valerian species, only the carefully processed roots of the *Valeriana officinalis* have been widely studied. However, not all studies have shown valerian to be effective, and there may be some dangers."

Another class of foods is those that increase melatonin, a brain chemical that produces sleep onset (the sleepy hormone). Tart cherry juice gets the most frequent mention of this class of foods. Walnuts and almonds contain melatonin, and cheese contains tryptophan.

The bottom line is that whether a food or drink increases tryptophan or melatonin, or induces other chemical changes, the effects of these so-called sleepy foods tend to be minimal. They may, however, also be just enough to promote falling asleep more quickly, particularly when paired with the placebo or psychological aspect of a bedtime routine that signals it's time to relax and sleep, with fewer side effects than sleeping pills.

STEP 3: MAGNESIUM SUPPLEMENTATION

Magnesium is the fourth-most abundant mineral in the human body and is critical to a healthy body and brain. It is estimated that 50 percent of the population is deficient in magnesium due to its depletion in our soil and to diets low in this mineral.

Sixty percent of magnesium is found in one's bones, and the rest resides in muscle and soft tissue. It is in every cell of your body and necessary to function. Magnesium is involved in more than six hundred reactions in the body, particularly converting food into energy. Magnesium deficiency can result in fatigue, muscle pain, and heart arrhythmia. Magnesium strengthens muscles, builds bones, energizes the brain, regulates the heart, reduces blood pressure, balances blood sugar, aids sleep, eases pain, improves digestion, and helps your body utilize calcium and absorb vitamin D. We used to consume 600 milligrams of magnesium daily but get only about 275 milligrams today, well below the 420 milligrams for men and 320 milligrams for women, depending on absorption rate, particularly in older individuals. The standard U.S. diet contains only about 50 percent of the recommended daily allowance.

The dosage of magnesium that will aid sleeplessness is different for each person; it ranges from 300 to 400 milligrams per day. A lab evaluation can help to determine whether magnesium levels are low and magnesium supplements or bananas, green leafy vegetables, nuts, or other foods rich in magnesium will help.

Some research indicates magnesium deficiency could impair exercise performance, since magnesium losses from intense sweat and urination could increase the magnesium requirement by 10–20 percent (Nielsen and Lukaski 2006).

Foods rich in magnesium are preferred over supplements, but if supplement magnesium is used, make sure to get a higher-quality lab-verified brand. Since the FDA does not regulate supplements, look for the label to have the "USP" dietary supplement certification, which means independent labs have verified the safety of and levels in the supplement.

Another important certification to look for on the outside label of a supplement is "GMP." The "good manufacturing practice" certification ensures that a system has been used to ensure products are consistently produced and controlled according to quality standards. It is designed to minimize any risks involved in production that cannot be eliminated by the final testing of the product—especially tainted fillers that can be toxic even in low doses.

The "USP" and "GMP" labels cover all aspects of production—materials, equipment, training, and personal hygiene of staff. Upscale supermarkets (Trader Joe's, Whole Foods) and high-end pharmacies tend to carry supplement products with these quality-control lab standards.

A number of small studies have shown that improved sleep quality associated with magnesium supplementation was most likely due to magnesium binding to GABA (gamma-aminobutyric acid) receptors. This process is similar to that of Ambien, Lunesta, and Sonata, the most widely prescribed sleeping medications. These medications have side effects and lose their effectiveness after prolonged use. They are well known to be difficult to ween oneself from. Ambien is prescribed for those who have difficulty falling asleep, as it is quick-acting, and Lunesta is given for those waking up in the middle of the night. It is important to know that the latest research indicates that these hypnotic medications add only eight to twenty minutes of sleep time per night, have many side effects, can be habit-forming if taken for more than a short period, and sometimes produce "rebound insomnia" if going off them too rapidly.

STEP 4: MELATONIN SUPPLEMENTATION

The next level of action for increasing sleep efficiency is the use of a popular supplement called melatonin. Melatonin is a hormone produced in the pineal gland that helps to regulate sleep and wake cycles. Your body produces melatonin naturally. Melatonin levels rise in the evening, and it promotes quiet wakefulness that promotes sleep, according to Dr. Luis Buenaver of Johns Hopkins.

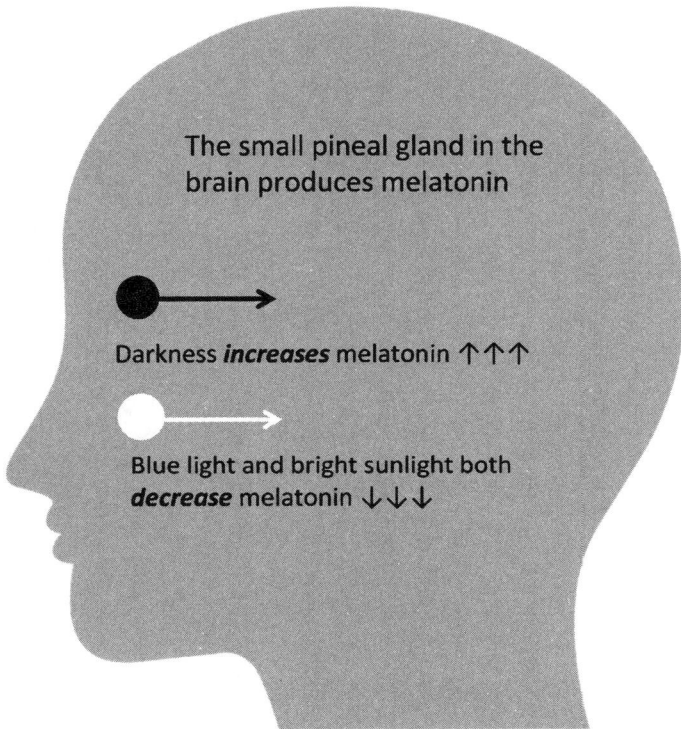

The small pineal gland in the brain produces melatonin

Darkness *increases* melatonin ↑↑↑

Blue light and bright sunlight both *decrease* melatonin ↓↓↓

Fig. 27. Melatonin. Created by Jack Stark.

Melatonin accumulates in the brain during waking hours, and our circadian rhythm, the internal clock that keeps the brain and body in sync with the sun, then releases it at the onset of darkness.

Darkness cues us to sleep by releasing melatonin.

Blue light (short wavelength), the kind that brightens midday's sunlight and is emitted by computers and smartphones, will shut off the release of melatonin (Finkel 2018).

Melatonin release—depending on the level of blue light that can disrupt and delay the release of melatonin—starts at around 9:30 p.m. and peaks between midnight and 5 a.m.

While most people produce enough melatonin on their own for sleep, if one is experiencing insomnia, jet lag, or other "sleep robbers," then supplementation with melatonin may be helpful. Jet lag is caused by flying in an airplane and crossing one or more time zones. The effects of jet lag are usually greater if you are going from the West Coast to the East Coast than from east to west. The symptoms of jet lag may take one or more days to go away. Melatonin may help reset your sleep and wake cycle. Take melatonin after dark the day you travel and after dark for a few days after arriving at your destination, and a few days before if you are flying eastward.

Melatonin sleep aids are growing in popularity, with 3 million Americans using them (Lelak et al. 2022). Supplementation may help a Top Gun performer fall asleep faster and regulate sleeping patterns, particularly with jet lag. Dosage is one to three milligrams two hours before bedtime. It is not recommended to exceed three milligrams, as a groggy feeling in the morning may impact performance.

It is best not to use melatonin on an ongoing basis or if you are pregnant or breastfeeding, or have an autoimmune disorder or depression.

We highly recommend purchasing a quality brand that has been lab verified, such as USP and MSP, and is free of yeast, gluten, preservatives, artificial flavors, and color additives. Many sanctioning bodies don't allow teams to give melatonin, magnesium, or GABA directly to athletes who are tested, not because of effectiveness but due to liability issues and worries about product contamination. That is why medical or pharmaceutical-grade lab-tested products should be used. Some sanctioning bodies have committees staffed with volunteers unfamiliar with these products that are essential to our daily bodily functioning. This is unfortunate, as the alternatives are not healthy.

STEP 5: GABA, THE HOT NEW PRODUCT

GABA (gamma-aminobutyric acid) is the hot new product for insomnia, particularly among functional-medicine physicians and professional sports teams. GABA is a chemical messenger that is widely distributed in the brain. Its function is to reduce the activity of the neurons to which it binds, which allows for the control of fear and anxiety when neurons are overexcited.

The inhibitory and calming action slows down signals between neurons and allows for brain and muscle relaxation. Certain foods that are high in GABA are also those that increase magnesium levels.

GABA supplements are now available in liquid form, and since GABA is a naturally occurring brain chemical, it is not prohibited by the NCAA or profes-

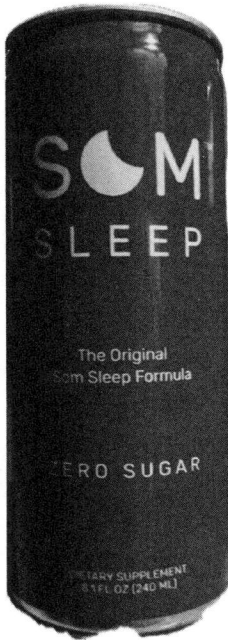

Fig. 28. Som Sleep. Courtesy Jack Stark.

sional teams. But many products that are cleared by the NCAA may need to be purchased by student athletes, as schools are not always allowed to distribute supplements without a prescription.

A new product in liquid form, used particularly by NBA teams because of their late-night travel between cities, is called Som Sleep. The container in which this over-the-counter product is sold looks like a soda can, but it contains all the natural products that promote sleep: (1) magnesium, (2) vitamin B6, (3) L-theanine (found in green tea), (4) melatonin, and (5) GABA. This liquid form of GABA is taken one hour to a half hour before bedtime. The cost per can is about $2.50. There are virtually no side effects in comparison with prescription medication.

STEP 6: OVER-THE-COUNTER AND PRESCRIPTION MEDICATION

Benadryl and other antihistamines should seldom be used to promote sleep as they tend to produce early-morning drowsiness. Tylenol PM, Advil PM, and NyQuil are over-the-counter pills that should be used for only a few nights at a time. Yet 41 percent of people use these pills for a year or longer, and 20 percent have even longer-term use. These medications contain diphenhydr-amine, an antihistamine used to shut down melatonin and is responsible for 450 deaths a year in overdoses. These pills also contain acetaminophen, a pain reliever effective at lower doses, which has a well-established history of causing both short-term and long-term liver damage and failure when used at very high doses exceeding three thousand milligrams a day. The U.S. Acute Liver Failure Study Group revealed 50 percent of all acute liver failures in the United States are from this drug, and 8–10 percent of cases have end-stage kidney disease with long-term use.

Antidepressants. Among the antidepressant medications used for insomnia, trazadone (Desyrel) is best at treating sleeplessness.

Benzodiazepines. Also called "benzos," they are an older class of drugs that stay in the system longer but can be addictive and are less effective after a short period. Xanax (alprazolam) is an example of this type of medication.

Hypnotics. The popular Sonata, Ambien, and Lunesta all help people fall asleep fast, but many wake up in the middle of the night. These medications produce grogginess the next day, are hard to get off of, and lose their effec-tiveness over time.

Always avoid alcohol with *all* sleep aids.

In summary, the more natural products that are low in side effects and high in effectiveness over time are the best options for busy Top Gun performers.

Daily Sleep Plan

Top Gun performers will want to develop a daily sleep plan to maximize energy and recover from demanding schedules. Listed below is a recommended plan to follow to get your zzzs.

9:00 p.m.: Reduce sleep disruptors
Caffeine (no. 1 abused drug in the world)
Alcohol
Obsessive worrying
Overstimulation
Electronic devices

Follow sleep-improvement tips

11:00 p.m.: Sleep guidelines

Cold

Dark

Wet

CPAP if needed

Presleep hygiene

Cognitive-behavior techniques

Routine schedules

Sleep enhancers: Add each step as needed

Step 1: Listen to "Deep Sleep" audio

Step 2: Eat sleepy foods

Step 3: Consider magnesium supplementation

Step 4: Consider melatonin supplementation

Step 5: Consider GABA capsule or liquid enhancement

Step 6: Prescription medications only if needed and then occasionally

3:00 a.m.: Insomnia—middle of the night

Reduce obsessive worries, utilize "Deep Sleep" audio file, and evaluate for depression

If necessary, get up and read—but quiet the mind

5:00 a.m.: Early-morning waking up

May require evaluation of sleep enhancers by using a higher-level intervention

Better to have a noon workout to get that deeper and extra hour of sleep

7:00 a.m.: Wake up

Keep a consistent wake-up time even on weekends

Immediate exposure to bright sunlight will charge your body and shut down that tired feeling and prepare you for an energized day

Following a consistent daily sleep plan can significantly increase a Top Gun performer's productivity in a world where the extra 5 percent is a difference maker.

PART 4

THE TOP GUN PROGRAM

11

Top Gun Application—School

Know thyself

Greek: Gnothi seauton

Latin: Nosce te ipsum

The ancient Greek aphorism "Know thyself" was inscribed above the entrance to the temple of Apollo in the ancient Greek precinct of Delphi.

It served as a moral principle and was one of the most important guides to life. Greeks would travel great distances to this holy temple to listen to the Delphic Oracle's prophecies about their most important concerns.

These concerns are centered not only on the *past* and the *present* but also, most important, *future* prophecies. What should one do regarding war and other great challenges in living their best lives?

The basis of all decisions was first to *know thyself.*

Do you really know yourself?

What is your purpose in life?

Why are you here?

And most important—How do you live life to your maximum potential?

How do you become a Top Gun performer?

In part 1 the authors shared their experience and their need, today more than ever, to be a Top Gun performer. The world is desperately in need of such leaders, and being such a leader will become only more challenging in the technology-driven world of the future. In part 2 the authors shared their experience in the three major phases of life: education (school), free time (sports), and work. Part 3 provided a deep analysis of guides that readers can download onto their phones—audio files that help maximize their performance in their journey through all phases of life. They empower readers to be in charge of their own destiny. Part 4 provides a more specific and summarized application in each of the phases of life to best *know thyself.*

Mental Health Challenges

Concerns about our youth are centuries old. Yet today our research reveals an unprecedented level of mental health issues among our youth.

The National Institute of Health's recent research indicates 42 percent of individuals aged fifteen to thirty exhibit levels of stress and anxiety that could be classified as a diagnosed mental illness. The younger generation is lonelier and more reluctant to embrace the responsibilities and joys of adulthood. Approximately half are or have recently been living with parents or relatives.

This explosion in the need for mental health services has overwhelmed our national system, resulting in a severe shortage of professionals in the field. The causes are fourfold:

social media and the internet,
iPhones and other smart phones ("iGen" is a term coined for the first generation to grow up using iPhones),
COVID-19 in the early 2020s and its impact for a decade, and
bullying, exacerbated by all of the above.

The iGen age group exhibits higher rates of suicide, depression, and pessimism since studies began in 1950. For example, rates of anxiety, depression, and suicide have doubled in the past twenty years. The sharpest rates of increase have been among teenage girls, especially those admitted to emergency rooms for self-harm.

The American Academy of Pediatrics recommends physicians screen all individuals between the ages of twelve and twenty for depression annually.

Half of all lifetime mental illness begins at the average age of fourteen, and 75 percent of cases begin by age twenty-four. Suicide is one of the leading causes of death among this age group in most states.

Treatment Concerns

The American system for supporting mental health has never been strong. The 2008 Mental Health Parity and Addiction Equity Act *did* help expand coverage, but it is extremely difficult to get insurance coverage to pay for more than a handful of outpatient sessions, and it is even more difficult to get coverage for inpatient treatment.

Inpatient psychiatric care (hospital beds) has been disappearing at an alarming rate due to the lack of payment for such services. It's almost impossible to deliver quality mental health care to the particularly chronic mentally ill and break even financially, as most facilities lose money or are subsidized privately.

The shift of mental health services over the past thirty years from inpatient care to community services has been a failure. The closing of state- and city-supported facilities resulted in financial savings, but the money never followed those in need. Homelessness resulted, and now our prisons have inherited the problem.

In state prison systems across the country, 56 percent of those incarcerated have mental illness and 16 percent of those have acute to severe mental illness. New prisons being built today have dedicated large sections for only those with severe mental health disorders.

Diagnosis Concerns

The process of diagnosing mental health behaviors has always been a concern, because there are no laboratory tests that can definitely say a person has a specific disorder. Diagnosis is subjective and can vary from one professional to another. Up to 40 percent of mild to moderate disorders are misdiagnosed.

In addition to the difficulty of diagnosing these behaviors is the use of medication. Primary care physicians are in short supply and are often pushed to see thirty to forty patients a day. Most patients have office visits of fifteen minutes, as there are so many patients to see. It is a challenge to totally understand these complex issues in a short amount of time.

Primary care doctors prescribe 90 percent of benzodiazepines (calming meds such as Valium, Xanax, and Ativan), 80 percent of antidepressants, 65 percent of ADHD meds, and 50 percent of antipsychotics. The result can too often be an overprescription of meds for the Mild and Mild-Moderate group that are not as closely monitored as they need to be.

Individuals aged fifteen to thirty are on the meds too long and are not tapered off properly (Frances 2013).

The Mental Health Model of Dysfunction

World health data have for decades recorded the top-two health issues most responsible for death—heart disease and cancer. While these will most likely continue as the main causes of *mortality*, the statistic misses the greatest health challenge of *morbidity*—mental health. Mental health far surpasses the impact of those diseases on the world in terms of cost, quality of life, and productivity, and it at least indirectly has links to heart disease and cancer.

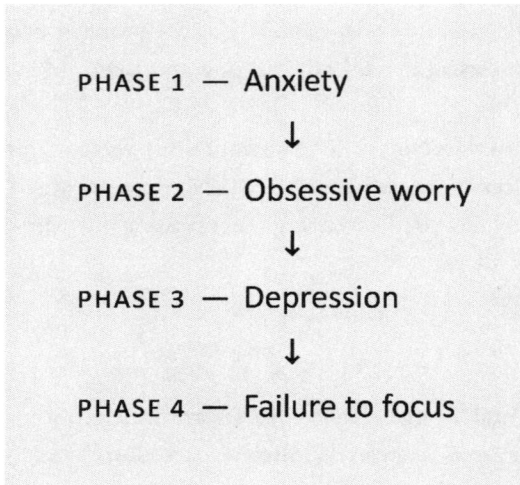

PHASE 1 — Anxiety

↓

PHASE 2 — Obsessive worry

↓

PHASE 3 — Depression

↓

PHASE 4 — Failure to focus

Fig. 29. The dysfunctional stages of worry. Created by Jack Stark.

THE DYSFUNCTION MODEL

Phase 1. We wake up early each day, and our minds begin to review what we need to get done. The overwhelming challenges, for half the population, can quickly spin them into a state of mild to moderately high anxiety. The traditional treatment approach is the use of antianxiety medication such as Klonopin, Xanax, and Prozac.

The challenges here are the side effects and the need to use them for only short periods of time while alternative techniques can be learned via psychotherapy and relaxation strategies.

Phase 2. By noon, if our anxiety continues to engulf us, we can find ourselves caught in a spinning cycle of obsessive worry—brought on by outside events but mostly controlled by our obsessive rumination and worry. If we get *nine* compliments in a day (never happens) and only one criticism (usually the reverse), what do we dwell on? Yes, the one criticism. We have become a world of worrywarts and perfectionists. Perhaps it's due to the fear of one bad tweet, one slip of the tongue, or an innocent comment or sociopolitical expression and the social media critics find a reason to attack us.

Phase 3. By the afternoon this spinning process alters our biophysiology, and we exhibit mild to severe symptoms of depression—difficulty thinking, fatigue, withdrawal, isolation, loss or excessive gain of appetite, and sleep disruption.

The quick answer has been a pill, which takes only seconds, versus the demanding work of self-control learned through therapy and training. Today new data suggests that the effectiveness of our sixty-plus-year-old model of antidepressants is being severely challenged as being no better than psychotherapy or exercise for 80 percent of the population.

Phase 4. By late afternoon and evening, the spinning can cause us to lose concentration and focus, resulting in withdrawal and overwhelming exhaustion from severe insomnia. Faced with this dysfunctional "whirlpool" pulling us down, we need a specific process of what to do at each phase of this daily challenge.

WHAT TO DO

We live in a world of daily complex demands, and the students, athletes, patients, pilots, and overwhelmed employees need answers as to what to do, when to do it, and how it will best help them. We read books, listen to podcasts, attend presentations, and they all help. But everyone can use simple, step-by-step assistance in "what to do when" in each of the three areas of our life: school, sports (free time), and work. The last three chapters will address each of these three areas and specify steps to follow.

Breaking the Anxiety Loop

The included audio files "Performance Relaxation" and "Instant Focus" are particularly useful in that educational period of our life—the first 20–30 percent of life, or ages fifteen to thirty years. They are also fundamental to building on being a Top Gun performer in school, sports, and work. Follow the summary below for maximum performance.

1. Performance Relaxation

APPLICATION: *Generalized anxiety.* Feeling anxious throughout the day across various settings and situations for which you fear you can't continue.

USE: It's best to use this audio file twice a day for thirty days to master the ability to control your anxiety. Taper off as needed.

IMPACT: In nine minutes this audio file will slow your heart rate, decrease your breathing, calm your mind, and sharpen your focus.

Situations
School attendance
Social gatherings
School activities
Performance situations

PERFORMANCE RELAXATION: PROCESS

Find a quiet, comfortable place where you can focus on the audio file; clear your mind so you can focus. Follow the directions of slowing your thoughts, becoming internally quiet, relaxing your muscles, visualizing yourself letting go, and focusing your mind on performing your best.

2. Instant Focus

APPLICATION: *Situational anxiety.* Specific situations that cause instant stressful reactions. *Panic attack.* Overwhelming anxiety resulting in a lack of physical and emotional control.

USE: Practice as frequently as needed until you have mastered control of your breathing while avoiding hyperventilation (rapid shallow breathing).

IMPACT: This eight-minute audio file provides instant focus and relaxation, allowing you to perform the task required at a higher level.

Situations
Stage fright
Test anxiety
Solo performance

INSTANT FOCUS: PROCESS

Most of us take our breathing for granted. It's an automatic bodily process that we repeat up to thirty thousand times a day. Breathing is a complex process involving muscles, blood vessels, the lungs, the heart, and the brain, and most of us do it incorrectly. Notice when infants breathe, it appears that their stomach goes up and down as if to fill it with their oxygen. We are born belly breathers (diaphragmatic breathers), and we become "shallow breathers" and worse, shallow and shoulder breathers. This results in a lack of maximum oxygen, which can stress and hinder our ability to function efficiently. Stress disorder costs $300 billion a year in health care and missed work.

When we breathe too shallowly, we use only the top third of our lungs. The bottom two-thirds of our lungs supply our best breathing capacity. Deep breathing comes naturally to children, but we lose the ability because we're in constant state of "fight or flight" low-level stress. A shallow breath is an anxious breath and can easily wear one out.

Panic attacks are often triggered by rapid shallow breaths, resulting in hyperventilation without our realizing it. Diaphragmatic breathing is a quick way to abort the panic or anxiety attacks.

There are two types of breathing.

1. Diaphragmatic breathing: the traditional method, thousands of years old, introduced by Eastern philosophers.
2. Tactical breathing: the second type, introduced by the Navy Seals, is best used in panic situations when you feel yourself having a fight-or-flight response (panic attacks).

Diaphragmatic breath. Find a comfortable place to lie down or sit in an upright chair, close your eyes, clear your mind, and breathe in through your nose, as doing so moistens and warms the air, purifying the breath as it goes into the body, and then breathe out through your mouth. You can start with a *cleansing breath*—breathe in very slowly, counting to eight seconds first by filling your abdomen. Put your hands on your belly and see your stomach fill up while inhaling for four seconds; then continue four more seconds, filling your chest. Slowly release the chest air, counting down to four, and count four more seconds while your stomach slowly come down. This process cleanses your entire system.

Then do your regular four seconds in and four seconds down over the next seven minutes.

Close with repeating another eight-second cleansing breath. You may feel as if you just took a pill, and your hands may begin to tingle as blood rushes in (a sign of relaxing). You will feel relaxed and may note a big drop in your heart rate.

Tactical breathing. Slightly different from diaphragmatic breathing, tactical breathing begins by placing your hand on your belly, pushing out with a big exhale. Then breathe in through your nostrils, slowly drawing the breath upward from your belly to your upper chest.

Pause and exhale, starting from your chest and moving downward to the lower part of your belly. Imagine your belly button touching your spine.

Repeat the deep breath and make the exhale twice as long as the length of the inhale. For example, inhale to the count of four, pause briefly, and exhale to the count of eight. Repeat three times (Kerr and McLanahan 2020).

12

Top Gun Application—Sports

Everyone has a plan—until they get punched in the mouth.
—MIKE TYSON

When life is going well for Americans, it becomes easy to feel confident, think positive thoughts, and be optimistic about the future. But as soon as we receive an unexpected setback, our minds are flooded with negative thoughts, anger, and stress (Zinsser 2022).

Is it time for a mental health makeover? Gaining mastery over your own mind is key to a healthy and happy life.

Staying Positive with a Negative Brain

Our mind is a tool that few of us ever learn how to use properly. A person has, on average, seventy thousand thoughts in a day—and the *negative thoughts* are three times more frequent than the *positive thoughts*. Why is it that one critical comment from a friend, one minor play in a game is enough to spoil our entire day? Why do our minds seem to focus on and place more importance on bad things instead of good things?

Research indicates that we have a negative bias which we tend to focus on, learn from, and use to protect ourselves. The evolutionary part of our brain protected us from impulsive decisions by reminding us there is danger in the world. The reason this negative bias exists is that we each have our own set of beliefs, ideas, notions, and experiences that color how we view the world around us.

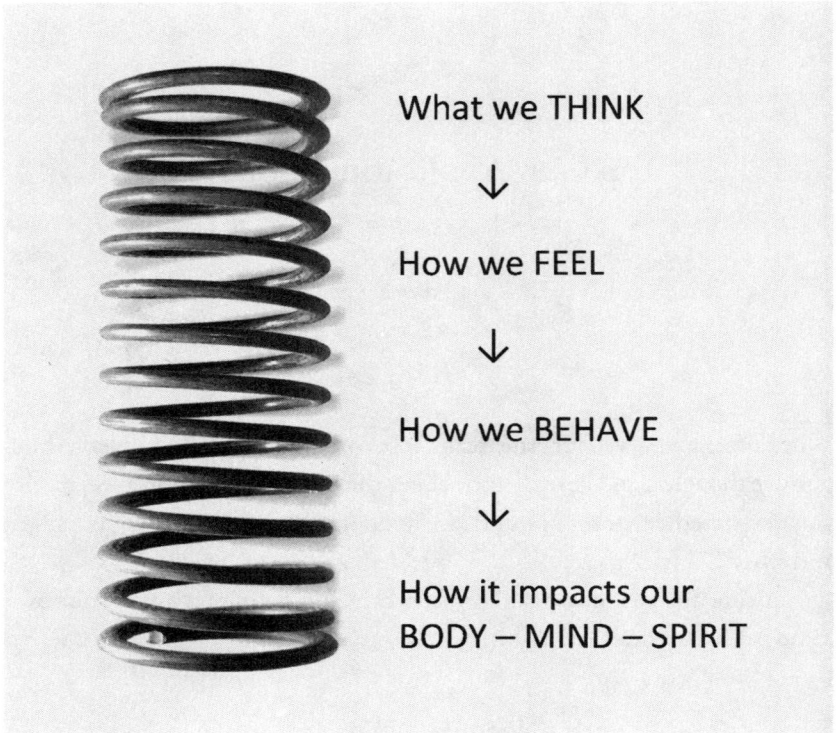

What we THINK

↓

How we FEEL

↓

How we BEHAVE

↓

How it impacts our
BODY – MIND – SPIRIT

Fig. 30. The worry spiral. Created by Jack Stark.

Negative Chatter in Our Head

What we think can, within seconds, cause a release of the stress hormone cortisol (adrenaline), impacting how we feel and then behave with consequences for our health—mind-body-spirit.

Ethan Kross, an experimental psychologist who specializes in emotional regulation, said this in his book *Chatter: The Voice in Our Head, Why It Matters, and How to Harness It*: "We talk to ourselves when we're trying to control ourselves or when we are trying to solve a problem. When we are doing something different, we mentally walk ourselves through the steps we need to take.

"Self-talk helps us to author the stories of our life, to capture stories that explain what we have gone through. We can learn from painful experiences that help us grow and improve."

Kross's research at his Emotion and Self-Control Laboratory indicated that we spend between a third and a half of our waking hours not focused on the present. Most of this time we are talking silently to ourselves.

Our inner speech—thinking—is the equivalent of speaking four thousand words per minute aloud. This is the equivalent of one hour of a presentation to us.

We worry, ruminate, or catastrophize. We get stuck and start to spin in our negativity, and this self-perpetuating spin causes us to spiral into a negative loop.

The major finding from hundreds of studies is that when people are feeling negative, they think differently than when they are feeling and thinking positively.

When athletes and high performers feel positive, they focus on the *forest*, not the *trees*. When they feel negative, they're all about the *trees*. Each of those viewpoints can be beneficial at different times.

Separating from Our Thoughts

A radical shift in perspective is required if we are to free ourselves from rumination. We need to recognize that thinking is something we do rather than something that we are. By acting as a listener, we can learn to engage only with thoughts that are helpful.

Research indicates that 95 percent of our thoughts are negative, and 90 percent are repetitive. Most self-help books direct us to change the negative to positive thoughts, but the content of our thoughts is not the issue. It's how we react to those thoughts that harm our performance.

3. Self-Talks +/- in the Zone

APPLICATION: *Obsessive worry and rumination.* Obsessive worry can sabotage our focus and wreak havoc on our bodies. Negative thinking within one second can bring about a cascade of hundreds of harmful changes in our body.

USE: This audio file is designed as an instructional guide to learn the technique of controlling one's negative thoughts. After a few dozen listening sessions, you can learn this self-control technique. You can use this audio file as a reference or as an occasional reminder.

IMPACT: The ten-minute audio file is designed to teach you a technique to block the negative self-talk loop and increase focus for optimal performance (see chapter 7 for a deeper guide).

Practice in a quiet place that allows you to learn this technique, and then apply it throughout the day across settings so that it becomes a natural habit.

Situations

Before practice and competition.

Daily affirmations to prevent fatigue and poor self-concept and to promote optimism.

Prevent mental blocks, "choking," slumps, and periods of poor performance.

SELF-TALKS: PROCESS

Audio file 3, "In the Zone," teaches each Top Gun performer to:

Stop negative rumination by interrupting the brain with the rubber band technique of snapping your wrist or clicking your fingers to halt the obsessive worry; shift to a pleasant mental place in your mind; or obsess on a powerful, joyful process—for example, winning the lottery, an award for performance, or recognition of your behavior.

Catch the "wrong loop" before it takes over and use coping techniques of positive self-talk.

Engage in *gratitude* thinking—focus on all the good things you have in life and be thankful. Research indicates that gratitude can be a powerful way to change one's attitude and behavior. Giving thanks boosts mental, emotional, and physical health, according to Gregory Jantz, author of *Healing Depression for Life* and *The Anxiety Reset*.

Recognize the dangers of perfectionism—25 percent of individuals ages twelve to thirty are highly perfectionist.

Control engagement with social media. The CDC reports on the profound impact of social media on all of us, especially youth, who are vulnerable to a spike in deaths by suicide. Tech devices are programmed via algorithms that produce addictive behaviors (fueled by surges in dopamine, a neurotransmitter in the brain) and has resulted in an alarming explosion of anger, violence, and intolerance in this country.

If more intense treatment is needed to extinguish this addictive and destructive behavior, the best recommendation is cognitive behavior therapy, the standard of treatment. Designed to change our cognition—how we think—and thereby change our behavior, this therapeutic technique was developed by Aaron Beck, an influential psychologist. Unlike Freudian psychoanalysis, which delves into a person's childhood and searches for hidden internal conflicts, cognitive therapy focuses on turning around a self-disparaging inner monologue—a key to alleviating many psychological problems, often in a dozen or fewer sessions.

Visualization

Audio file 4, "Visualization," focuses on this critical skill. Why is this particular skill one of the six most important in academics, sports, and work? All performance metrics depend on one's ability to "see" where one is and where to go to best perform and be the best in class. The visualization audio file is designed to sharpen your visual skills by taking you through five steps (see chapter 8).

Visualization is particularly effective at improving performance by reducing fears (phobias) and depression. By using the psychological technique of systematic desensitization, fears are decreased by breaking down a behavior into smaller steps and then, step by step, desensitizing a person to that fear until it is gradually eliminated.

Depression is often accompanied by a sense of helplessness and hopelessness. Performers get stuck. A vision of what they can be and guided imagery to help them get there are powerful tools.

Staggering Research Findings

A new survey by Gallup of the world's emotional state showed that Americans are among the most negative people on the planet, with a level of negativity even higher than that during the Great Depression. According to Gallup, 64 percent of Americans between the ages of fifteen and thirty and 65 percent of those between the ages of thirty and fifty are stressed a lot. Anger, loneliness, violence, and sadness have resulted in a staggering impact on our nation, with no letup in sight.

In addition to the benefits of self-training, these chapters and audio files offer one of the most powerful tools to be a Top Gun performer.

The journal *Global Advances in Health and Medicine* has published a growing body of evidence that exercising is a powerful tool when it comes to battling depression, anxiety, and performance outcomes, even stronger than medication in 80 percent of the cases.

New research (meta-analysis) linked inflammation as a major contributor to the development of depression and other mood disorders. Blood samples of depressed patients showed elevated ranges of inflammatory biomarkers.

By reducing inflammation through exercise, individuals (all but the more severely inflamed who may also need medication and other treatments) find that exercise mediates the activity of serotonin receptors, which are associated with an antidepressant effect.

Early in my career, I was treating a group of twenty older teenagers referred for their mental health issues. The one-hour group therapy sessions were just okay for outcomes, but it was slow. So, I added one-hour sessions of weight-lifting and running. I was stunned at the progress and improvement of the group's behavior in a short period.

Two thousand steps each day
= 8 percent drop in all deaths
= 11 percent drop in cancer deaths
= 10 percent drop in heart deaths

An eight-year study of four hundred thousand individuals showed that fifteen minutes of exercise had even better health outcomes (*Lancet*).

Swimmer Michael Phelps was the most decorated Olympian ever. It is doubtful that anyone will ever match his swimming accomplishments. But at one time in his life, Phelps locked himself in his bedroom for four days. He had just been arrested a second time for driving while under the influence. (Alcohol has long been used inappropriately as a "medication" for depression.) He was lost, questioned life despite all his success, and contemplated suicide. He attributed his recovery to his family, friends, and a support group.

A Visit to the National Helen Keller Institute

Early in my career, I had the opportunity to work with families who had a child with visual and auditory impairment. Many such cases were the result of a rubella epidemic while the mothers were pregnant.

I was invited to speak at the Helen Keller National Center for Deaf/Blind Youths and Adults in Manhattan, New York City. My first visit to New York via the subway system was inspiring and humbling. It was inspiring because I observed individuals who could neither see nor hear compensate via sign language into a person's hand, with Braille chips inserted under their skin to help them "hear" what I was saying. They were learning visualization skills via touch (tactile) training. How blessed I was to be able to learn so easily!

And it was humbling. As I finished my presentation, I realized I had forgotten how to get back to the correct subway platform. The CEO had an enthusiastic sense of humor and suggested that Mary Ann could take me to the train platform. I took Mary Ann's arm, and she, using her cane, guided me to the exact spot and time for my return to my hotel. This "hotshot PhD" was intimidated by the neighborhood and how to find his way back. Mary Ann just smiled and waved goodbye.

Characteristics of a Top Athlete

In addition to the material in this chapter, our years of experience and research indicate a profile of personality characteristics and mental skills that will allow athletes to be most successful.

Confidence: High self-concept and self-esteem. Assurance of one's own abilities.

Coachability: Understanding and responding to instruction. Attentive and willing to follow directions.

Self-Motivation: An intrinsic desire to prepare and compete at an elevated level all of the time. An enjoyment of the sport.

Competitiveness: An inclination to compete, a sense of rivalry and aggression, and a strong need for victory.

Work Ethic/Persistence: An understanding of the importance of practice and dedication. An ability to continue to prepare and perform hard through all situations.

Team Player: An obligation to the team as a whole. An understanding of the necessity of team cohesiveness.

Concentration: Ability to focus. Ability to learn and retain material-cognitive skills.

Mental Stability: Emotional balance. Abilities to avoid drugs and alcohol and to control mental health problems.

4. Visualization

APPLICATION: Visualization is effective in preventing or reducing phobias—fear of failure—particularly in competition activities ranging from exercise to elite athletic events. Visualization skills rank at the top for high performance activities while reducing the helplessness and hopelessness symptoms of depression.

USE: Critique your visual skills to measure your level of performance by enhancing your maximum level through frequent practice until it becomes a natural part of your daily life. This is a training and instructional audio file to use as a tune-up after you have mastered this skill set.

IMPACT: This ten-minute audio file provides visual enhancement to help with decision making and eye-hand coordination in competition.

VISUALIZATION: PROCESS

Practice use of this audio file until it becomes a learned skill that you can use throughout the day across various settings.

Step 1: Body Scan
Step 2: Relaxation Breathing
Step 3: Progressive Muscle Relaxation
Step 4: Sensory Awareness
Step 5: Visualize Your Best Performance

13

Top Gun Application—Work

A person once asked the Dalai Lama, "What surprises you most about humanity?" The Dalai Lama answered, "Man! Because he sacrifices his health in order to make money. Then he sacrifices money to recuperate his health. And then he is so anxious about the future that he does not enjoy the present; the result being that he does not live in the present or the future; he lives as if he is never going to die, and then dies having never really lived."

Watch your thoughts, for they become words. Choose your words, for they become actions. Understand your actions, for they become habits. Study your habits, for they become your character. Develop your character, for it becomes your destiny.

—ANONYMOUS

Becoming a Top Gun performer in the last two-thirds of one's life is the focus of this chapter. After school and perhaps sports as a career or as part of your lifestyle comes your calling. What do you want to do with your life? Your dream, your job, your work, your "boardroom" experience.

Two of the tools for you to have an exceptional accomplishment in work are the focus of self-hypnosis and deep sleep, two traits beneficial to one's success along with the other four audio files.

The authors of this book (a decorated military leader and a performance psychologist) draw on their experiences. One was in the military as a Top Gun pilot who went on to lead the training of those attending the War College, the Naval Academy, and two Big Ten universities; the other has been a consultant to more than one hundred corporations. Both have made thousands of presentations on leadership issues to corporations and learned much via their own training and being mentored along the way.

The "Work" in this chapter's title represents life after your school career and competitive sports, whether it be at home with your family or in the workplace with its demanding requirements.

The self-hypnosis audio file is designed to both increase performance across all areas of your life and remove any trauma you acquired along life's journey.

5. Hypnosis—Peak Performance

APPLICATION: Effective at removing traumatic experiences in the past including those of people with diagnoses of post-traumatic stress disorder. In addition, it is a powerful tool to aid with classroom work, athletic performance, and stress-related work.

USE: Use this fourteen-minute audio file just before competition, stressful situations at home, or work requiring exceptional performance with a clear, calm mind and focused vision.

IMPACT: This audio file will calm the mind and body, sharpen your focus on the immediate task requiring a Top Gun performance, and shed all doubts to allow a clear vision for performing your best.

Deep Sleep

Ask any teacher, coach, or boss if they could have only one wish to squeeze that last 5 percent of performance from their students, players, or employees, and their unanimous response would be SLEEP!

FOR STUDENTS

Time management is the biggest challenge for those individuals between ages thirteen and thirty who have varying sleeping needs and schedules and have a hard time adjusting to the rigid schedules of academics.

Sleep records reveal a high correlation between sleep quality and exceptional grades. The data is clear that "pulling all-nighters" does not consistently help with retaining information and performing well on tests.

FOR ATHLETES

The demands on athletes between school and up to thirty hours a week for elite high school, college, and pro players require consistent discipline. Superstar athletes follow a rigid adherence to nine or more hours of sleep each night to manage the extraordinary demands on their bodies.

College and pro teams spend enormous amounts of money on nutritionists, exercise physiologists, and especially sleep aids.

That 5 percent difference means not finishing in the middle of the conference but winning a state or national championship. Flying F-4 Phantoms at Mach+ speed requires alertness in missions involving dogfights to dodging surface-to-air missiles. Most dogfights are high-intensity, heart-pounding, fearfully focused events lasting only minutes.

Sleep deprivation was a critical factor in the biggest loss of a top-five-ranked football team in the school's history. Nebraska football had just beaten the number three team in the country, was playing Iowa State away, and was a twenty-seven-point favorite. I saw the team captain just before the game, and he looked exhausted, as though he had not slept all night. I thought he was sick. I asked what was wrong, and he said he had pulled a couple of all-nighters during the past few days for midterm exams. He was an engineering major. He assured me he, along with the team, would be okay in a couple of hours.

I told the Hall of Fame coach Tom Osborne that the players were tired but would be okay by game time. His answer startled me: "We'd better be because if we aren't, we could get beat." I silently thought, "No way! We are twenty-seven-point favorites, and it will be easy." Wow! Was I wrong. We lost the game, and it wasn't close. We looked slow—like we were running in wet cement. It was the biggest win for the opponent, as they had not beaten us in decades.

The following season I asked the head coach if I could speak to the team. His response was, "Well, it must be important for you to request ten minutes with the team during a busy week!" Gulp! I shared with the team that I had done an analysis of the team's performance on the eighth and ninth weeks of each season for the previous ten years.

Each year those weeks coincided with midsemester exams, and although we won almost all the games, our performance during those weeks was the worst of the season. I shared what had happened the year before, especially among the older students who were majoring in engineering, pre-law, or pre-med, many of whom were used to cramming by staying up late during that week.

To my surprise, Coach Osborne called the entire team to huddle around him right after practice that day. He stated, "I just want to emphasize the importance of what Jack said in our team meeting. Today is Tuesday, and you need to get your sleep starting tonight and every night this week."

There were no all-nighters for exams, and we won by four touchdowns that week. Perhaps it made a difference.

The "Deep Sleep" audio file is designed to augment your sleep.

6. Deep Sleep

APPLICATION: *Insomnia and sleep apnea.* Sleep disorders can have a profound impact on one's performance throughout life. Both mental health and physical health, particularly heart disease and immunity issues, are impacted by sleep deprivation.

USE: Use this audio file on an as-needed basis. The best part is that there are no side effects or cost—and you have full control of the outcome.

IMPACT: This nine-minute audio file is designed to enhance deeper sleep by quieting the mind, shutting off outside worries, and focusing on slowly inducing the initial stages of sleep. If early morning wakeup occurs, you can play the audio file again. As you are about to drift off, you can shut off the recording. Track your quality and quantity of sleep and use the stacking techniques listed below to guarantee a deeper night's sleep. Use each step until you are able to sleep soundly.

DEEP SLEEP: PROCESS

Cold. A cool room temperature of sixty to seventy degrees, depending on comfort, facilitates a deeper sleep.

Dark. Total darkness tells the brain to secrete the natural hormone melatonin. Turn off all "blue" lights on TVs, computers, iPads, tablets, and cell phones.

Wet. To create a moist room, particularly in a dry location, use a humidifier and a small hygrometer device indicating levels of humidity for comfortable sleep.

Use CPAP machine. For sleep apnea, which has a major health impact on brain and heart functioning.

Presleep hygiene. Ensure a quiet room and a clean, comfortable bed, brush your teeth, et cetera.

Routine schedule. Set times to go to sleep and to wake up. Maintain a consistent pattern for each night.

Sleep disruptors. Avoid caffeine, antidepressants, smoking, alcohol, and stimulating activities after 6 p.m.

Sleep enhancers. Stacking techniques—add each step below until you reach your desired level of optimal sleep.

Step 1: "Deep Sleep" audio file.

Step 2: Sleepy foods. Avoid sugar and emphasize protein. (See the complete list in chapter 10.)

Step 3: Magnesium supplementation via food or supplements. Always make sure any supplements have either the label "USP," certifying safety in the levels of the supplement and any added "fillers," or the "GMP" (good manufacturing practice) label, assuring quality manufacturing standards are met. While USP and GMP certification offers some assurance about a supplement's safety, the National Institute of Health's Office of Dietary Supplements provides information that should not take the place of medical advice (https://ods.od.nih.gov/). Also consult the National Center for Complementary and Integrative Health (https://www.nccih.nih.gov/).

We encourage you to talk to your health care providers (physician, MD; registered dietician, RD; pharmacist, PharmD). Supplements may interfere with some prescription medications and vice versa; for instance, statins like Lipitor and Crestor are known to deplete COQ10, a powerful antioxidant.

Step 4: Melatonin—recommended three-milligram dose to avoid early-morning grogginess and not to be used for a prolonged period. Some over-the-counter sales have five- and ten-milligram tablets, which may be too much. Sales have tripled in the past few years.

Step 5: GABA as a supplement or in a drink. GABA is an inhibitory neurotransmitter found naturally in the brain and in certain foods that

reduce brain activity, promote calmness, and aid sleep. Consult with
experts on its use also.

Step 6: Avoid using prescription sleep medications such as Lunesta,
Ambien, and Sonata on a long-term basis, or benzodiazepines such as
Xanax and Ativan.

Countdown to Your Best Night's Sleep

8 hours before bedtime: Stop use of caffeine, as it takes eight hours to
exit your body.

3 hours before bedtime: Stop exercising—exercise increases body
temperature.

2 hours before bedtime: Stop eating; avoid indigestion issues.

1.5 hours before bedtime: Turn off all electronic screens. Wavelengths of
light emitted by TVs, smart phones, tablets, and computer screens can
interfere with circadian rhythms, making sleep difficult.

1.5 hours before bedtime: Use melatonin or other supplements. They take
90 minutes to work best, as just before bedtime is too late.

1.5 hours before bedtime: Turn down the thermostat to obtain a room
temperature of sixty to seventy degrees, depending on your comfort
zone.

1 hour before bedtime: Stop intake of all liquids. Avoid sleep interrup-
tion due to the need to urinate. Organize for next day with clothes,
et cetera.

40 minutes before bedtime: Take care of night hygiene; avoid bright
bathroom lights.

20 minutes before bedtime: Engage in little to no physical activity by listening to music, relaxing, reading, meditating, and so forth (Michael
Breus, PhD, Fellow, American Academy of Sleep Medicine, and
author of *The Power of When: Discover Your Chronotype*).

Appendix

Six Mental Skills—Audio Files

1. Performance Relaxation
https://audio.tgperf.com/audio-one

2. Instant Focus
https://audio.tgperf.com/audio-two

3. Self-Talks +/- in the Zone
https://audio.tgperf.com/audio-three

4. Visualization
https://audio.tgperf.com/audio-four

5. Hypnosis—Peak Performance
https://audio.tgperf.com/audio-five

6. Deep Sleep
https://audio.tgperf.com/audio-six

References

Akerstedt, T., and P. M. Nilsson. 2003. "Sleep as Restitution: An Introduction." *Journal of Internal Medicine* 254 (1): 6–12.

Anderson, Clare, and James A. Horne. 2006. "Sleepiness Enhances Distraction during a Monotonous Task." *Sleep* 29 (4): 573–76.

Anspaugh, David, dir. 1986. *Hoosiers*. Cinema '84, Hemdale.

Arntz, A. 2012. "Imagery Rescripting as a Therapeutic Technique: Review of Clinical Trials, Basic Studied and Research Agenda." *Journal of Experimental Psychopathology* 3: 121–26.

Bacon, Lloyd, dir. 1940. *Knute Rockne—All-American*. Warner Brothers.

Beck, A. T. 1967. *Depression: Causes and Treatment*. Philadelphia: University of Pennsylvania Press.

Bonnet, M. H. 2005. "Sleep Deprivation." In *Principles and Practice of Sleep Medicine*, edited by M. H. Kryger, T. Roth, and W. C. Dement, 55. 4th ed. Philadelphia: Elsevier Saunders.

Breus, Michael. 2016. *The Power of When: Discover Your Chronotype—and the Best Time to Eat Lunch, Ask for a Raise, Have Sex, Write a Novel, Take Your Meds, and More*. Little, Brown Spark.

Brewer, B. W., M. B. Andersen, and J. L. Van Raalte. 2002. "Psychological Aspects of Sport Injury Rehabilitation: Toward a Biopsychosocial Approach." In *Medical and Psychological Aspects of Sport and Exercise*, edited by D. L. Mostofsky and L. D. Zaichkowsky, 41–54. Morgantown WV: Fitness Information Technology.

Cajochen. C., K. Kräuchi, and A. Wirz-Justice. 2003. "Role of Melatonin in the Regulation of Human Circadian Rhythms and Sleep." *Journal of Neuroendocrinology* 15 (4): 432–37.

Carton, A. M., and B. J. Lucas. 2018. "How Can Leaders Overcome the Blurry Vision Bias? Identifying an Antidote to the Paradox of Vision Communication." *Academy of Management Journal* 61 (6). https://doi.org/10.5465/amj.2015.0375.

Catley, D., and J. Duda. 1997. "Psychological Antecedents of the Frequency and Intensity of Flow in Golfers." *International Journal of Sport Psychology* 28: 309–22.

Cohn, P. 1991. "An Exploratory Study of Peak Performance in Golf." *Sport Psychologist* 5: 1–14.

Del Casale, A., S. Ferracuti, C. Rapinesi, D. Serata, G. Sani, V. Savoja, G. D. Kotzalidis, R. Tatarelli, and P. Girardi. 2012. "Neurocognition under Hypnosis: Findings from Recent Functional Neuroimaging Studies." *International Journal of Clinical and Experimental Hypnosis* 60 (3): 286–317. https://doi.org/10.1080/00207144.2012.675295.

Driskell, J. E., C. Copper, and A. Moran. 1994. "Does Mental Practice Enhance Performance?" *Journal of Applied Psychology* 79: 481–91.

Dunlap, E. M. 2005. "Hypnotizability among Division-I Athletes." PhD diss., University of Idaho, Moscow.

Dworsky, D., and V. Krane. n.d. "Using the Mind to Heal the Body: Imagery for Injury Rehabilitation." Association for Applied Sport Psychology. Accessed September 20, 2009. https://appliedsportpsych.org/resources/injury-rehabilitation/using-the-mind -to-heal-the-body-imagery-for-injury-rehabilitation/.

Ehring, T., and E. R. Watkins. 2008. "Repetitive Negative Thinking as a Transdiagnostic Process." *International Journal of Cognitive Therapy* 1: 192–205.

Ericsson, K. Anders, and Paul Ward. 2007. "Capturing the Naturally Occurring Superior Performance of Experts in the Laboratory: Toward a Science of Expert and Exceptional Performance." *Current Directions in Psychological Science* 16 (6). https://doi .org/10.1111/j.1467-8721.2007.00533.x.

Fields, Douglas. 2016. *Why We Snap: Understanding the Rage Circuit in Your Brain.* Dutton.

Finkel, Michael. 2018. "Want to Fall Asleep? Read This Story." *National Geographic*, August, pp. 40–79.

Floyd, Ronnie W. 2018. *Living Fit: Make Your Life Count by Pursuing a Healthy You.* B&H Books.

Frances, Allen. 2013. *Essentials of Psychiatric Diagnosis: Responding to the Challenge of DSM-5.* Rev. ed. Guilford Press.

Fullagar, H. K., S. Skorski, R. Duffield, D. Hammes, A. J. Coutts, and T. Meyer. 2015. "Sleep and Athletic Performance: The Effects of Sleep Loss on Exercise Performance, and Physiological and Cognitive Responses to Exercise." *Sports Medicine* 45 (2): 161– 86. https://doi.org/10.1007/s40279-014-0260-0.

Garver, R. B. 1990. "Suggestions for Studying, Concentration and Test Anxiety." In *Handbook of Hypnotic Suggestions and Metaphors*, edited by D. Corydon Hammond, 445. New York: W. W. Norton.

Goodwin, Doris Kearns. 2018. "Lincoln and the Art of Transformative Leadership." *Harvard Business Review*, September–October. https://hbr.org/2018/09/lincoln -and-the-art-of-transformative-leadership.

Gould, D., C. Greenleaf, and V. Krane. 2002. "Arousal-Anxiety and Sport Behavior." In *Advances in Sport Psychology*, edited by T. Horn, 207–41. 2nd ed. Champaign IL: Human Kinetics.

Gould, D., D. Feltz, T. Horn, and M. Weiss. 1982. "Reasons for Discontinuing Involvement in Competitive Youth Swimming." *Journal of Sport Behavior* 5: 155–65.

Gould, D., R. Ecklund, and S. Jackson. 1992. "1988 U.S. Olympic Wrestling Excellence: II. Thoughts and Attitudes Occurring during Competition." *Sport Psychologist* 6: 383–402.

Gould, D., S. Jackson, and L. Finch. 1993. "Sources of Stress in National Champion Figure Skaters." *Journal of Sport and Exercise Psychology* 15: 134–59.

Graham, Jennifer. 2017. "Why Is Everyone So Angry and How Can We Change That?" *Deseret News*, July 19.

Halson, S. L. 2014. "Sleep in Elite Athletes and Nutritional Interventions to Enhance Sleep." *Sports Medicine* 44 (Suppl 1): s13–s23. https://doi.org/10.1007/s40279-014-0147-0.

Juliff, L. E., S. L. Halson, and J. J. Peiffer. 2014. "Understanding Sleep Disturbance in Athletes Prior to Important Competitions." *Journal of Science and Medicine in Sport*, February 13.

Kavanu, J. L. 1997. "The Origin and Evolution of Sleep: Roles of Vision and Endothermy." *Brain Research Bulletin* 42: 245–64.

Kerr, Meera Patricia, and Sandra A. McLanahan. 2020. *Take a Deep Breath: A Simple Exercise Guide to Increasing Your Oxygen Intake*. Square One.

Kingsley, Christine. 2024. "Lung Capacity: What You Need to Know." Lung Institute. https://lunginstitute.com/lung-capacity/.

Klumpers, U. M. H., D. J. Veltman, M.-J. van Tol, R. W. Kloet, R. Boellaard, A. A. Lammertsma, and W. J. G. Hoogendijk. 2015. "Neurophysiological Effects of Sleep Deprivation in Healthy Adults: A Pilot Study." *PloS ONE* 10 (1). https://doi.org/10.1371/journal.pone.0116906.

Kong, D., C.-S. Soon, and M. W. L. Chee. 2011. "Reduced Visual Processing Capacity in Sleep-Deprived Persons." *NeuroImage* 55: 629–34. https://doi.org/10.1016/j.neuroimage.2010.12.057.

Krenz, E. W., R. Gordin, and S. W. Edwards. 1985. "Effects of Hypnosis on State Anxiety and Stress in Male and Female Intercollegiate Athletes." In *Modern Trends in Hypnosis*, edited by D. Waxman, P. C. Misra, M. Gibson, and M. A. Basker. Boston: Springer.

Kross, Ethan. 2021. *Chatter: The Voice in Our Head, Why It Matters, and How to Harness It*. Crown.

Land, W. M., C. Frank, and T. Schack. 2014. "The Influence of Attentional Focus on the Development of Skill Representation in a Complex Action." *Psychology of Sport and Exercise* 15: 30–38. https://doi.org/10.1016/j.psychsport.2013.09.006.

Leeder, J., M. Glaister, K. Pizzoferro, et al. 2012. "Sleep Duration and Quality in Elite Athletes Measured Using Wristwatch Actigraphy." *Journal of Sports Science* 30 (6): 541–45.

Lelak, K., V. Vohra, M I. Neuman, M. S. Toce, and U. Sethuraman. 2022. "Pediatric Melatonin Ingestions—United States, 2012–2021." *Morbidity and Mortality Weekly Report* 71: 725–29. https://dx.doi.org/10.15585/mmwr.mm7122a1.

Leslie, Mitch. 2000. "Research Supports the Notion That Hypnosis Can Transform Perception." *Stanford Report*, September 6.

Lyubomirsky, S., and C. Tkach. 2004. "The Consequences of Dysphoric Rumination." In *Depressive Rumination: Nature, Theory, and Treatments*, edited by C. Papageorgiou and A. Wells, 21–42. London: Wiley.

Mah, C. D., K. E. Mah, E. J. Kezirian, and W. C. Dement. 2011. "The Effects of Sleep Extension on the Athletic Performance of Collegiate Basketball Players." *Sleep* 34 (7): 943–50.

Mahoney, M. J., and M. Avener. 1977. "Psychology of the Elite Athlete: An Exploratory Study." *Cognitive Therapy and Research* 1 (2): 135–41. https://doi.org/10.1007/BF01173634.

Maynard, I., M. Smith, and L. Warwick-Evans. 1995. "The Effects of a Cognitive Intervention Strategy on Competitive State Anxiety and Performance in Semiprofessional Soccer Players." *Journal of Sport and Exercise Psychology* 17: 428–46.

McEvoy, P. M., M. L. Moulds, and A. E. J. Mahoney. 2014. "Repetitive Negative Thinking in Anticipation of a Stressor." *Behaviour Change* 31 (1): 18–33. https://doi.org/10.1017/bec.2013.30.

Metzger, R. L., M. L. Miller, M. Cohen, M. Sofka, and T. D. Borkovec. 1990. "Worry Changes Decision Making: The Effect of Negative Thoughts on Cognitive Processing." *Journal of Clinical Psychology* 46: 78–88. https://doi.org/10.1002/1097-4679(199001)46:1<78::AID-JCLP2270460113>3.0.CO;2-R.

Miller, Gregory, Edith Chen, and Karen Parker. 2017. "Why Death Haunts Black Lives." *Proceedings of the National Academy of Science* 114 (5): 800–802.

Milling, L. S., and E. S. Randazzo. 2016. "Enhancing Sports Performance with Hypnosis: An Ode for Tiger Woods." *Psychology of Consciousness: Theory, Research, and Practice* 3 (1): 45–60. https://doi.org/10.1037/cns0000055.

Nédélec, M., S. Halson, B. Delecroix, A. Abaidia, S. Ahmaidi, and G. Dupont. 2015. "Sleep Hygiene and Recovery Strategies in Elite Soccer Players." *Sports Medicine* 45 (11): 1547–59. https://doi.org/10.1007/s40279-015-0377-9.

Nielsen, F. H., and H. C. Lukaski. 2006. "Update on the Relationship between Magnesium and Exercise." *Magnesium Research* 19 (3): 180–89.

Nolen-Hoeksema, S. 1991. "Responses to Depression and Their Effects on the Duration of Depressive Episodes." *Journal of Abnormal Psychology* 100: 569–82.

Nowack, K. 2017. "Sleep, Emotional Intelligence, and Interpersonal Effectiveness: Natural Bedfellows." *Consulting Psychology Journal: Practice and Research* 69 (2): 66–79. https://doi.org/10.1037/cpb0000077.

O'Brian, C. 2011. "Empower Your Athletic Abilities." *USA Today Magazine* 139 (2792): 54.

Orma, Steve. 2015. *Stop Worrying and Go to Sleep: How to Put Insomnia to Bed for Good.* Published by author.

Pates, J. 2013. "The Effects of Hypnosis on an Elite Senior European Tour Golfer: A Single-Subject Design." *International Journal of Clinical and Experimental Hypnosis* 61 (2): 193–204. https://doi.org/10.1080/00207144.2013.753831.

Pates, J. K., and I. Maynard. 2000. "Effects of Hypnosis on Flow States and Golf Performance." *Perceptual and Motor Skills* 91: 1057–75.

Pates, J. K., R. Oliver, and I. Maynard. 2001. "The Effects of Hypnosis on Flow States and Golf Putting Performance." *Journal of Applied Sport Psychology* 13: 341–54.

Pearce, M. 1997. "Hypnosis and Imagination Visualization." *Australian Journal of Clinical Hypnotherapy and Hypnosis* 18 (1): 33–38.

Pham, Lien B., and Shelley E. Taylor. 1999. "From Thought to Action: Effects of Process- Versus Outcome-Based Mental Simulations on Performance." *Personality and Social Psychology Bulletin* 25 (2): 250–60.

Rahman, S. A., C. M. Shapiro, F. Wang, H. Ainlay, S. Kazmi, T. J. Brown, and R. F. Casper. 2013. "Effects of Filtering Visual Short Wavelengths during Nocturnal Shiftwork on Sleep and Performance." *Chronobiology International* 30 (8): 951–62.

Rama, Swami, Rudolph Ballentine, and Alan Hymes. 1998. *Science of Breath: A Practical Guide*. Himalyan Institute Press.

Reilly, T., and T. Deykin. 1983. "Effects of Partial Sleep Loss on Subjective States, Psychomotor, and Physical Performance Tests." *Journal of Human Movement Studies* 9: 157–70.

Scanlan, T. K., M. L. Babkes, and L. A. Scanlan. 2005. "Participation in Sport: A Developmental Glimpse at Emotion." In *Organized Activities as Contexts of Development: Extracurricular Activities, After-School, and Community Programs*, edited by J. L. Mahoney, R. W. Larson, and J. S. Eccles. Mahwah NJ: Lawrence Erlbaum.

Schichl, M., M. Ziberi, O. Lahl, and R. Pietrowsky. 2011. "The Influence of Midday Naps and Relaxation-Hypnosis on Declarative and Procedural Memory Performance." *Sleep and Hypnosis* 13 (1–2): 8–14.

Schmidt, Richard A., Timothy D. Lee, Carolee J. Winstein, Gabriele Wulf, and Howard N. Zelaznik. 2017. *Motor Control and Learning: A Behavior Emphasis*. 6th ed. Human Kinetics.

Schreiber, E. H. 1991. "Using Hypnosis to Improve Performance of College Basketball Players." *Perceptual and Motor Skills* 72 (2): 536–38. https://doi.org/10.2466/PMS .72.2.536-538.

Slimani, M., K. Chamari, D. Boudhiba, and F. Cheour. 2016. "Mediator and Moderator Variables of Imagery Use-Motor Learning and Sport Performance Relationships: A Narrative Review." *Sport Sciences for Health* 12: 1–9.

Smith, R. E., and F. L. Smoll. 1991. "Behavioral Research and Intervention in Youth Sports." *Behavior Therapy* 22: 329–44.

Smith, R. E., F. L. Smoll, and M. W. Passer. 2002. "Sport Performance Anxiety in Young Athletes." In *Children and Youth in Sport: A Biopsychosocial Perspective*, edited by F. L. Smoll and R. E. Smith, 501–36. 2nd ed. Dubuque IA: Kendall/Hunt.

Social Isolation and Loneliness in Older Adults: Opportunities for the Health Care System. 2020. Consensus Study Report. National Academies of Sciences, Engineering, and Medicine.

Stepanski, Edward J., and James K. Wyatt. "Use of Sleep Hygiene in the Treatment of Insomnia." *Sleep Medicine Reviews* 7 (3): 215–25. https://doi.org/10.1053/smrv .2001.0246.

Stickgold, R. "Sleep-Dependent Memory Consolidation." *Nature* 437: 1272–78.

Stone, Oliver, dir. 1999. *Any Given Sunday*. Warner Brothers.

Suinn, Richard M. 1986. *Seven Steps to Peak Performance*. Lewiston NY: Hans Huber.

Tkachenko, Olga, Elizabeth A. Olson, Mareen Weber, Lily A. Preer, Hannah Gogel, and William D. S. Kilgore. 2014. "Sleep Difficulties Are Associated with Increased Symptoms of Psychopathology." *Experimental Brain Research* 232 (5): 1567–74. https://doi.org/10.1007/s00221-014-3827-y.

Whitbourne, Susan. 2010. "Is Our Society Getting Increasingly Angry?" *Psychology Today*, October 12.

Wiese-Bjornstal, D. M., A. M. Smith, S. M. Shaffer, and M. A. Morrey. 1998. "An Integrated Model of Response to Sport Injury: Psychological and Sociological Dimensions." *Journal of Applied Sport Psychology* 10: 46–69.

Wong, S. S. 2012. "Negative Thinking versus Positive Thinking in a Singaporean Student Sample: Relationships with Psychological Well-Being and Psychological Maladjustment." *Learning and Individual Differences* 22 (1): 76–82. https://doi.org/10.1016 /j.lindif.2011.11.013.

Zhao, Yujie, Liu Yang, Barbara J. Sahakian, et al. 2023. "The Brain Structure, Immunometabolic and Genetic Mechanism Underlying the Association between Lifestyle and Depression." *Nature Mental Health* 1 (10): 736–50. https://doi.org/10.1038 /s44220-023-00120-1.

Zinsser, Nate. 2022. *The Confident Mind: A Battle-Tested Guide to Unshakable Performance*. Harper Collins.

Index